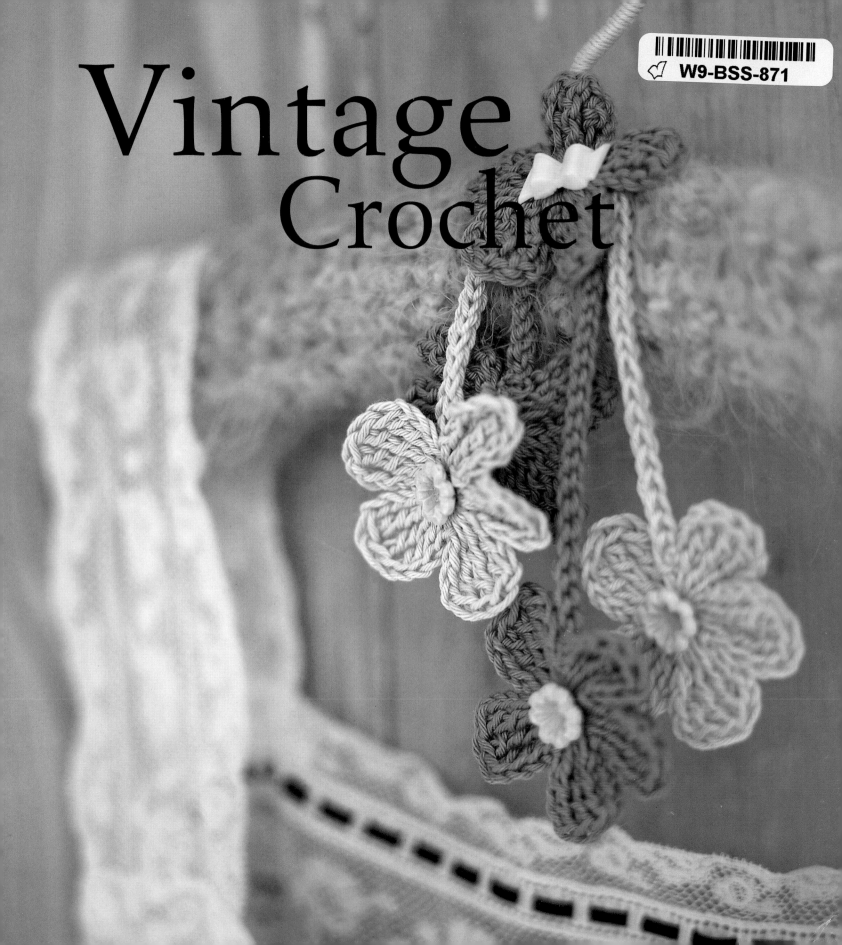

Vintage Crochet

Vintage Crochet

30 Gorgeous Designs for Home • Garden • Fashion • Gifts

Susan Cropper

photography by Kristin Perers

Watson-Guptill Publications / New York

First published in 2007 in the United States by
Watson-Guptill Publications,
Nielsen Business Media,
a division of The Nielsen Company
770 Broadway, New York, NY 10003
www.watsonguptill.com

Text and patterns copyright
        © 2007 by Susan Cropper
Photography, design, and layout copyright
        © 2007 by Jacqui Small

ISBN-10: 0-8230-9976-8
ISBN-13: 978-0-8230-9976-4

Library of Congress Control Number:
2007930017

Printed in China

First printing, 2007

1 2 3 4 5 / 11 10 09 08 07

Contents

Introduction

To me, the word "vintage" evokes slightly wistful emotions, inspired by the delightful combination of character and charm that's enhanced by an object's past use. The word is imbued with something intangible—it conjures up cabins in the woods, canoes by a lake, cowslip-covered fields, swallows, the moody light of early morning, twilight on snow, candles, and fairy lights.

These are some of the things that have inspired the patterns in this book. In their individual styles, each contributing designer has created a modern take on "vintage." which is also playful, cozy, beautiful, and slightly quirky. Any one of these designs would sit as happily in—or look as gorgeous on you in—a snow-covered mountain cabin as in a stylish city apartment. Colors, too, can evoke these feelings, so we have worked in a sensitive palette of duck-egg blue, mauve, pale green, burnt orange, moose brown, fig, and pale peach.

When I first dreamed of opening my London shop, Loop, it was crucial to me that it be a place full of charm and beauty—a warm and welcoming space where people could come to be inspired, as well as to browse, buy, talk, and learn. As a knitter and self-confessed yarn junkie, I had found it frustrating that there was no shop in the city that reflected the exciting new developments taking place in the world of knitting and crochet. Yarn outlets sold only a very limited selection of the breathtaking array of yarns that are now available, and there was nowhere offering practical workshops on all aspects of knitting and crochet, along with knitted or crocheted garments, homeware, and quirky toys and accessories created by the wealth of talented young designers that are working in fiber. So, this is what I set out to achieve with Loop. Above all, I wanted it to be a space where everything to do with knitting and crochet was available under one roof—from vintage buttons and useful and unusual notions, to a varied selection of yarns, patterns, and books, and to workshops, as well as the finished work of some of the most creative independent designers and makers.

Now, two years later, the shelves are filled with yarns from around the world. We stock everything from the simplest basic natural yarn to the kookiest hand-dyed hand-spuns. My passion for fiber, texture, and color never seems to wane, and one thing that drives me is my wish to pass on this enthusiasm to others and inspire them to create beautiful things. From the simplest crocheted scarf to the most

elaborate garment or throw—it is all possible with the same basic tools: a crochet hook and a length of yarn (or ribbon, or strips of fabric knotted together, or anything else you may wish to experiment with). That's all you need to create these amazing things—and, really, how cool is that?

It has been such an honor for me, through Loop, to meet a host of creative young designers who have reclaimed this traditional craft and stamped it with their unique sense of style. Their work is an inspiration and a cause to celebrate. All of the designers who have contributed patterns to this book have a connection to Loop in one way or another. Some are designers or designer-makers, whose wonderful patterns, yarn, or finished work we sell; others work in the shop or teach the classes. I have the most enormous respect for them all, and collaborating with them—both at Loop and in the making of this book—continues to be a joy.

Most of the patterns are fairly straightforward and require only basic to intermediate crochet skills—ideal for beginner crocheters, who just need a little nudge to try out shaping or new stitches. Others, such as Kristeen Griffin-Grimes's "Betty" Shrug (see pages 36-41) or Leigh Radford's exquisite Papillon Canopy (see pages 84-7), are quite challenging. Both of these will demand patience and dedication, but the results will be worth it—they are some of the things that have made us "ooh" and "aah" as the samples came in. There also other gorgeous items to wear—a dress, a wrap, and a cardigan, for example—and sweet accessories, such as a scarf, a headband, and a corsage. For a cozy modern-retro home there are pretty tablecloths, blankets, and the loveliest breakfast set embellished with vintage buttons.

The designers have written their patterns in their own style, but the directions are all clear, and there are step-by-step instructions for the trickier techniques (see pages 120-37). Once you set your heart on making one of the patterns, I suggest you read through it before you begin, to get a feeling for what is involved, and refer to the Techniques section if necessary. It's always a good idea to practice on a swatch to get to grips with the stitch and required gauge. Keep the swatch to refer to later, and start building a personal swatch library.

I hope you will feel inclined to make the patterns your own, too, by experimenting with different yarns, colors, and embellishments. Feel free to decorate items with beads, buttons, pompoms, and ribbons, as well as more unusual trims, such as lace flowers, charms, or strips of fabric.

Vintage Crochet is a little extension of Loop and those who make it special. We hope you love the patterns as much as we do and find some inspiration within these pages to make some pretty wonderful things for yourself and others. Happy crocheting!

Beautiful, Sumptuous Yarns

I feel sure that the resurgence in popularity of knitting and crochet in recent years is partly due to people being seduced by the huge variety of gorgeous yarns that are now available. Who wouldn't be? Yarn stores today are as beautiful and enticing as cake shops! The luscious array of colors offered—from mouthwatering hot pinks and oranges, rich berry purples, and vibrant greens to the soft, subtle shades of dusty lilacs, chalky blues, and muddy grays and browns—and the myriad textures—from the softest cashmere and fluffy angora, to smooth cotton and silk, to exquisite ribbon and sparkly yarn to nubbly hand-spuns—can make choosing just one a bewildering, if exhilarating, experience.

Beautiful yarns are what inspired me to open Loop; and this small space, with its lovely outdoor deck and cozy fireplace, now brims with more than 130 different yarns from all over the British Isles, North and South America, continental Europe, Australia, South Africa, and Japan. Each has its own soul and character, from pear tree's speckled fine merino, which is so divine it feels like cashmere, to Blue Sky Alpacas Alpaca Silk, with its gorgeous saturated colors and beautiful drape, to the subdued palette of Debbie Bliss yarns and the wonderful hand-dyed Bamboo yarn from Be Sweet—the choices are astounding. There is truly a sense of joy in sourcing the most exquisite and unique yarns. When I go to yarn trade fairs in Europe or the United States, I could swoon with delight as I wander along the endless aisles of merinos, mohair, hand-dyes, hand-spuns, bouclés, tweeds,

Left: There are many different textures of yarn available in gorgeous vintage hues, such as Blue Sky Alpacas "Melange," a divine 100% baby alpaca yarn with a heathered look, in shade 812 Blue Cheese (top); Blue Sky Alpacas "Alpaca Silk," 50% alpaca and 50% silk, in shade 136 Champagne (bottom left); and Lana Grossa "Royal Tweed," 100% fine merino, in shade 32 (bottom right).

Opposite: An array of crochet hooks from Clover, Balene, and Susan Bates. Vintage buttons are wonderful to collect and add instant character to a crocheted piece. Besides using them for fastenings, you can sew them on as an embellishment, along with velvet ribbon. These examples have been chosen to complement the rich color of Blue Sky Alpacas "Melange" in shade 807 Dijon.

ribbons, chenilles, bamboo, cashmere, alpacas, and silks. And I am always thrilled when I hear the exclamations of delight as people browse around the shop. It is a lovely moment, too, when a customer brings a new discovery into the shop to share with us—and sometimes those yarns end up on the shelves.

Yarn comes from animals (from goats to silkworms), from plants, and from synthetic materials. There is wool, merino, mohair, cashmere, alpaca, angora, silk, cotton, linen, hemp, paper, bamboo, acrylic, steel wrapped with silk, stainless-steel wire (which is particularly good for crocheted jewelry), and an endless variety of blends of these fibers available as yarn. Yarn from rare breeds, as well as hand-spun and hand-dyed, Fairtrade and organic yarns, are also growing in variety as well as accessibility. You can also experiment with tearing fabric into narrow strips and tying them together, then crocheting with the fabric "yarn." Bee Clinch's Picnic Blanket (on pages 72–5) is a delicious example of this. Vintage fabric or ribbon is great for this technique and works well as a lovely edging for a throw or blanket.

There are also many different weights of yarn. In Britain we have lace-weight, 4-ply, and double-knitting (DK); in the United States, their slightly heavier counterparts fingering, sportweight, and worsted weight—this last comparable to the British Aran weight. There are chunky and bulky yarns as well. In general, you can substitute one yarn for another, provided it is made of a similar fiber and can produce the same gauge. Make a swatch before you begin, though, as you may need to adjust your hook size.

There are many innovative independent yarn spinners and dyers producing unusual yarns and pushing the boundaries of what yarn can be. Among them are Gina Wilde, of Alchemy Yarns in California, who hand-paints silk, mohair, and bamboo; and Nadine Curtis, of Be Sweet, adding nubbiness, beads, and ribbons to her delicious colors of hand-dyed yarns from South Africa; Takako Ueki, of Habu, sourcing the most exquisite unusual yarns from small mills around Japan. There is also Lexi Boeger, of PluckyFluff, who hand-spins

Opposite: We've got stash! There are all kinds of yarns to choose from—including ggh "Amelie," a man-made fiber that feels like angora, as well as cashmere, silk, alpaca, felted merino, and ribbon yarns.

Right: Guv'nor, the dog, having fun messing around with ggh "Bel Air," a lovely lightly felted Aran-weight merino yarn in shade 19.

her yarn and throws in the most gorgeous combinations of felted flowers, beads, sequins, pompoms, buttons, cloth, and bobbles. Though somewhat too difficult to crochet anything substantial with, this type of yarn makes a great edging if worked with a large hook.

There has also been a great resurgence of people spinning and dyeing yarn in small cottage industries. The full list of people involved in these crafts is too long to give here, but the wide range, excellent quality, and sheer beauty of their yarns testify to the energy and excitement surrounding yarn today.

Whatever yarn you choose, always buy the best quality your budget allows. So much time goes into making the piece that your work deserves the best materials.

Dramatic oversized crochet motifs in the softest merino and silk yarn create an open, airy wrap worthy of a glamorous Hollywood star. Inspired by the signature style of silver-screen legend Ava Gardner, the "Ava" wrap is easily constructed, in one piece, in Louisa Harding's Grace yarn. This is a great intermediate project that will bring vintage pizzazz to any outfit.

"Ava" Wrap

Kristeen Griffin-Grimes for French Girl

MATERIALS

7 balls Louisa Harding Grace (DK, 50% silk, 50% merino wool, approx. 1⅜ oz/50g, 109⅜ yards/100m), shade 04 Powder
Size 5.5mm (1/9) crochet hook (see page 120)
Tapestry needle

MEASUREMENTS

Finished size (blocked): 20 x 80 inches (50 x 200cm).

GAUGE

One pattern repeat (18 sts) = 5¾ inches (14.6 cm) using a size 5.5mm (1/9) hook or the size required to obtain the correct gauge.

ABBREVIATIONS

See page 120.

WRAP

Ch 257.
Row 1: 1 dc into the 7th ch from hook * ch 1, skip 1 ch on foundation ch, 1 dc in next ch, repeat from * to end. This will leave 253 sts to work the main pattern into.

Main pattern

Row 2: Ch 6, skip 3 sts, * 1 tr in each of next 3 sts, ch 3, skip 3 sts, (1 tr, ch 3, 1 tr) in next st, ch 3, skip 3, 1 tr in each of next 3 sts, ch 5, skip 5 sts, repeat from * to 3 sts before end, ending with ch 2 instead of ch 5, 1 tr in last st. Turn.
Row 3: Ch 6, * 1 tr in each of next 3 tr from last row, ch 1, (1 tr, ch 1) 7 times into ch-3 sp, 1 tr in each of next 3 tr, ch 5, repeat from * to 3 sts before end, ending with ch 2 instead of ch 5, tr in 4th ch of

beginning ch-6 from row 2. Turn.

Row 4: Ch 5, * 1 tr in each of next 3 tr, ch 5, sc in ch st between first and 2nd tr, (ch 6, sc in next ch) 5 times, ch 5, 1 tr in each of next 3 tr, ch 3, repeat from * to 3 sts before end, ending with ch 1 instead of ch 3, place tr in last st (4th ch in beginning ch-6 from row 3). Turn.

Row 5: Ch 4, * 1 tr in each of next 3 tr, ch 5, sc into first ch-6 from last row. Continue to (ch 6, sc into ch-6 from last row) 4 times, then ch 5, place 1 tr in each of next tr, ch 1; repeat from * to end, eliminating ch 1, skip 1 st, place 1 tr into 4th ch in ch-5 from last row. Turn.

Row 6: Ch 4, place 1 tr in each of next 3 tr, * ch 5, sc into next ch-6 loop from last row. (Ch 6, sc into next ch-6 loop) 3 times, ch 5, place 1 tr in next 2 tr, tr2tog over next 2 tr, 1 tr in each of next 2 tr; repeat from * to 4 sts before end, ending with 1 tr in next 2 tr, tr2tog over last 2 sts. Turn.

Row 7: Ch 4, place 2 tr in each of next 2 tr, * ch 6, sc into 1st ch-6 from last row. (Ch 6, sc in next ch-6) twice, ch 6, place 1 tr in each of next 5 tr, repeat from * to 3 sts before end, ending with 3 tr in last 3 tr. Turn.

Row 8: Ch 4, skip first tr, place 1 tr in each of next 2 tr; * ch 7, sc into first ch-6 loop, ch 6, sc into next ch-6 loop, ch 7, place 1 tr in next 5 tr, repeat from * to 3 sts before end, ending with 3 tr instead of 5 tr. Turn.

Row 9: Ch 8, place 1 tr in each of next 3 tr, * ch 8, sc in ch-6 loop, ch 8, 1 tr in next 2 tr, then place (1 tr, ch 5, 1 tr) in next tr, 1 tr in each of next 2 tr, repeat from * to 3 sts before end, ending with 1 tr in next 2 tr, then [1 tr, ch 2, 1 dtr (wrap yo 3 times)] in last st (4th ch in ch-4 from row 8). Turn.

Row 10: Ch 6, tr into dtr from last row, ch 3, 1 tr into each of next 3 tr, * ch 7, place 1 tr in each of next 3 sts, ch 3, place (1 tr, ch-3, 1 tr) in ch-5 loop, ch 3, place 1 tr in each of next 3 sts, repeat from * to 3 sts before end, ending with ch 3, (1 tr, ch 1, 1 dtr) in 6th ch in ch-8 from last row. Turn.

Row 11: Ch 5, (1 tr, ch 1) 3 times into ch-1 from last row, * place 1 tr in each of next 3 tr, ch 5, place 1 tr in each of next 3 tr, ch 1, then (1 tr, ch 1) 7 times into ch-3 sp, 1 tr in each of next 3 tr, ch 5, repeat from * to 9 sts before end, ending with 1 tr in each of last 3 tr, ch 1, (1 tr, ch 1) 3 times, 1 tr into ch-6 loop from last row. Turn.

Row 12: Ch 7, sc in first ch-1 sp, (ch 6, sc into ch-1 sp) twice, ch 5, 1 tr in each of next 3 tr, ch 3, * place 1 tr in each of next 3 tr, ch 5, place sc in first ch st between first and 2nd tr, (ch 6, sc in next ch) 5 times, ch 5, 1 tr in each of next 3 tr, ch 3, repeat from *, ending with 1 tr in each of the last 3 tr, ch 5, sc in next ch-1 sp, (ch 6, sc into ch-1 sp) twice, ch 3, 1 tr into 4th ch of ch-5 from last row. Turn.

Row 13: Ch 1, sc into the top of tr from last row, ch 6, sc into ch-6 loop from last row, ch 6, sc into next ch-6 loop, ch 5, 1 tr in each of next 3 tr, ch 1, * 1 tr in each of next 3 tr, ch 5, (ch 6, sc into ch-6 loop from

last row) 4 times, then ch 5, place 1 tr in each of next tr, ch 1; repeat from * to end, ending with 1 tr in each of last 3 tr, ch 5, sc, into ch-6 loop from last row, (ch 6, sc into ch-6 loop) twice. Turn.

Row 14: Ch 7, sc in first ch-6 loop, ch 6, sc in next ch-6 loop, ch 5, * place 1 tr in next 2 tr, then tr2tog over next 2 tr, 1 tr in each of next 2 tr *ch 5, sc into next ch-6 loop from last row. (Ch 6, sc into next ch-6 loop) 3 times, ch 5; repeat from * to last 2 ch-6 loops from last row, ending with sc into 2nd-to-last ch-6 loop, ch 6, sc in next ch-6 loop, ch 3, 1 tr into sc at beginning of last row. Turn.

Row 15: Ch 1, sc into the top of tr from last row, ch 6, sc into ch-6 loop from last row, ch 6, * place 1 tr in each of next 5 tr, ch 6, sc into first ch-6 from last row, (ch 6, sc in next ch-6) twice, ch 6, repeat from * to last 2 loops, place (1 sc, ch 6, 1 sc) over last 2 loops. Turn.

Row 16: Ch 7, sc in ch-6 loop from last row, * ch 7, place 1 tr in next 5 tr, ch 7, sc into first ch-6 loop, ch 6, sc into next ch-6 loop, ch 7, place 1 tr in next 5 tr, repeat from * to last ch-6 loop, sc in ch-6 loop, ch 3, 1 tr into sc from beginning of last row. Turn.

Row 17: Ch 1, sc into the top of tr from last row, * ch 8, 1 tr in next 2 tr, then place (1 tr, ch 5, 1 tr) in next tr, 1 tr in next 2 tr, ch 8, sc into top of ch-6 loop, repeat from * to last loop. Turn.

Row 18: Ch 12, * 1 tr into each of next 3 tr, ch 3, place (1 tr, ch-3, 1 tr) in ch-5 loop, ch 3, place 1 tr in each of next 3 sts, ch 7, repeat from * last ch 7 ending with long tr, with yarn wrapped around hook 5 times, placed in sc from beginning of last row. Turn.

Rows 19–23: Repeat Rows 3–7.

FINISHING

Darn in all ends using a tapestry needle.

Pin out and block lightly by spraying with water (see page 137).

This shift dress is an adaptation of an original 1960s design. The bodice is worked in double crochet and the skirt in panels of "Irish" crochet motifs. The two sections are connected by a double crochet eyelet row threaded with matching ribbon. The skirt can be made longer or shorter by either adding or reducing the number of panels in the skirt.

"Nico" Dress

Bee Clinch

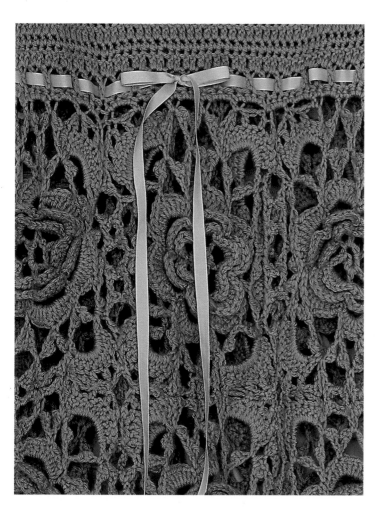

MATERIALS

10 balls Debbie Bliss Cashmerino Aran (55% merino wool, 33% microfiber, 12% cashmere, approx. 1¾ oz/50g, 98 yards/90m), shade 05 Smoky Blue
Size 5mm (H/8) crochet hook (see page 120)
Tapestry needle
1 yard (1m) matching satin ribbon, ½ inch (1cm) wide

MEASUREMENTS

One-size dress fits sizes 8-12.
Garment measurements: bust 37 inches (94cm); length of back bodice 11 inches (28cm); length of skirt 23 inches (58cm).

GAUGE

Each motif measures 7 x 7 inches (18 x 18cm).
18 sts to 4 inches (10cm) using a size 5mm (H/8) hook or the size required to obtain the correct gauge.

ABBREVIATIONS

See page 120.

NOTE

This dress is based on an orginal 1960s pattern, which comes in only one size; it can be worn either loose or close fitting and looks great both ways. Because it is made up of square motifs, the only way to size it up or down would be to add or reduce the number of motifs or panels in the skirt section.

SKIRT

To work a motif (make 18 in total): ch 8, sl st to beginning to form a ring.
Round 1: Ch 6 (counts as dc, ch 3), * 1 dc into circle, 3 ch; repeat from * 4 times, sl st to 3rd ch of 6 ch. 6 spaces.
Round 2: Into each sp work (1 sc, 1 hdc, 3 dc, 1 hdc, 1 sc) sl st to first sc. 6 petals.
Round 3: * Ch 5, 1 sc into next dc of round 1, inserting hook into the back of the stitch; repeat from * ending sl st to back of first sc.
Round 4: Into each sp work (1 sc, 1 hdc, 5 dc, 1 hdc, 1 sc), sl st to back of first sc.
Round 5: * Ch 7, 1 sc into next sc on round 3 inserting hook into stitch from back; repeat from * ending sl st to back of first sc.
Round 6: Into each sp work (1 sc, 1 hdc, 7 dc, 1 hdc, 1 sc), sl st to first sc.
Round 7: 1 sc into first sc on next petal * ch 4, 1 sc into 3rd ch from hook (picot made), ch 1, 1 sc into center dc of same petal (picot loop made), ** ch 4, 1 sc into 3rd ch from hook; repeat from ** once, ch 1, 1 sc into first sc on next petal; repeat from * omitting last sc and ending sl st into first sc.
Round 8: Sl st to center of first picot loop (between picots), 1 sc into same loop, * ch 7, 1 sc between picots on next picot loop, turn, ch 3, 9 dc into ch-7 loop, 1 dc into next sc, ch 4, turn, skip first 2 dc, 1 dc into next

dc, ** ch 1, skip 1 dc, 1 dc into next dc; repeat from ** twice more, ch 1, skip 1 dc, 1 dc into top of ch-3, ch 4, 1 sc into 3rd ch from hook, ch 1, 1 sc into same loop as sc after ch-7, *** ch 4, 1 sc into 3rd ch from hook, ch 4, 1 sc into 3rd ch from hook, ch 1, 1 sc between picots on next picot loop; repeat from *** once; repeat from * omitting last sc and ending sl st into first sc. Fasten off.

Finishing skirt

Pin out each square, making the center ch of the group the corner ch sp. Press lightly on the right side, leaving the center 4 rounds unpressed (first 2 rounds of petals).

Sew 9 squares together for front skirt (3 rows of 3 squares) and remaining 9 squares together for back skirt.

When sewing the squares together, use the picots and corner ch sps as joining points. The piece should still retain a lacelike appearance.

FRONT BODICE

With right side of front skirt facing and using hook, rejoin yarn to corner ch and work as follows.

Foundation row 1: 1 sc into corner ch sp * ch 3, skip ch-1 sp, 1 sc into next ch sp, ch 3, 1 sc into ch between the 2 picots, ch 3, 1 sc into ch between next 2 picots, ch 3, 1 sc into ch-4 loop, ch 3, skip ch-1 sp, 1 sc into corner ch sp of worked motif and next motif; repeat from * across other 2 motifs, ch 1, turn. 15 ch sps.

Foundation row 2: 1 sc into first sc, * 3 sc into ch sp, 1 sc into next sc; repeat from * 6 times (60 sts), ch 2, turn.

Now work in bodice pattern as follows.

Row 1 (eyelet row): 1 dc into first st, * ch 1, skip 1 st, 1 dc into next st; repeat from * to end, ch 1, turn.

Row 2 (and subsequent even rows): 1 sc into first st, sc to end, ch 2, turn.

Row 3 (and subsequent odd rows): 1 dc into first st, dc to end, ch 1, turn.

Work in patt until 14 rows in total have been worked (including eyelet row).

Armhole shaping

Row 1: Sl st 3, ch 3, dc to last 3 st, ch 1, turn. 54 sts.

Row 2: Sc to end, ch 2, turn.

Repeat first row of armhole shaping. 48 sts.

Continue in pattern with these sts until 16 rows in total have been worked since start of armhole shaping, finishing with an even-numbered row.

Left neck opening

Dc 12 sts, ch 1, turn. Sc to end.

Work straight for 6 more rows.

Left shoulder shaping

Row 1: Sl st 6, ch 2, dc to end, ch 1, turn.

Row 2: Sc to end. Fasten off.

Right neck opening

With right side facing, rejoin yarn 12 sts from right armhole edge, ch 2, dc to end, ch 1, turn.

Work straight for 7 more rows.

Repeat left shoulder shaping, reversing instructions.

BACK BODICE

Work as for front bodice, working 18 rows to neck shaping after armholes, finishing with an even-numbered row.

Left neck shaping

Work in pattern across 12 sts, ch 1, turn.

Work 3 rows straight.

Shape shoulder as given for front bodice.

Rejoin yarn for right side and work 3 rows; shape shoulder as for front bodice.

SLEEVES (Make 2)

Ch 40 + 1.

Row 1: Starting in 2nd ch from hook, sc to end, ch 2, turn.

Row 2: Starting in first st, dc to end, ch 1, turn.

Repeat these 2 rows 3 times. Total 8 rows

Armhole shaping

Row 1: Sl st 3, ch 2, sc to last 3 sts, ch 1, turn.

Row 2: Dc to end, ch 2, turn.

Rows 3–6: Repeat these 2 rows twice. 28 sts.

Row 7: Sl st 1 at beginning of next row, sc to 2nd st from end, ch 1, turn. 26 sts.

Row 8: Dc to end, ch 2, turn.

Row 9: Repeat last decrease row. 24 sts.

Row 10: Dc to end, ch 2, turn.

Upper sleeve shaping

Row 11: Sl st 6, sc to last 6 sts, ch 1, turn. 12 sts.

Row 12: Dc to end, ch 2, turn.

Row 13: Sl st 3, sc to last 3 st, ch 1, turn.

Row 14: Dc to end. Fasten off.

FINISHING

Press bodice (see page 137).

All bodice seams can be joined with sc. Join shoulder seams.

With right sides together insert sleeves into armhole arc.

Join side seams of motifs as described for the motif method. Join side seams of bodice.

Thread ribbon through eyelets.

Work 1 row of firm sc around neck, working 1 sc into each st or row end.

Crocheted in natural hand-spun organic cotton yarn, this "flower-child" tunic reminds us of summer days, daisy chains, and the sounds of buzzing bees and someone's radio playing in the distance.

"Joni" Flower Tunic Bobbi IntVeld

MATERIALS
12 (13, 14, 15) balls Blue Sky Alpacas Handspun Organic Cotton (DK, 100% organic cotton, approx. 2³⁄₈ oz/68g, 132 yards/120m, shade 60 Natural Cream
Size 3.75mm (F/5) crochet hook (see page 120)
Tapestry needle

MEASUREMENTS
To fit four sizes: S (M, L, XL).
Bust: 35 (39, 43, 47) inches (89 [99, 109, 119]cm).
Length: 25 (25½, 26, 26½) inches (64 [65, 66, 67]cm).
Sleeve length: 20½ (20½, 21, 21) inches (52 [52, 53, 53]cm).

NOTE
Instructions for larger sizes are given in parentheses. Where there is only one figure, it applies to all sizes.

GAUGE
Flower mesh pattern: 10 sts and 5 sps to 2 inches (5cm) using size 3.75mm (F/5) hook.
Single crochet band: 10 sc to 2 inches (5cm) using size 3.75mm (F/5) hook.
Crossed double crochet pattern: 10 cdc to 2 inches (5cm) using size 3.75mm (F/5) hook.
Change hook size if necessary to obtain correct gauge.

ABBREVIATIONS
See page 120.

SPECIAL ABBREVIATIONS
4lps–4-looped puff stitch: (Yo, insert hook into st, yo, draw up a loop, pulling slightly to make an elongated st) repeat 4 times (9 loops), yo, pull though all loops, ch 1. (See also page 123.)
cdc–crossed double crochet: Skip next st, dc into next st, dc into skipped st. (See also page 124.)

sc3tog: Work 3 sc without pulling through the last st, and then pull a loop through all the loops on the hook.

BACK
Ch 93 (113, 133, 153).
Flower mesh pattern
Row 1 (RS): Dc in 5th ch from hook, * ch 1, skip 1 ch, dc in next ch, * repeat to end, turn. 45 (55, 65, 75) sps.
Row 2 (WS): Ch 4, * dc in next dc, ch 1, * repeat to end, dc in 3rd turning ch, turn.
Row 3: Ch 4, dc in next dc, ch 1, * dc in next dc, work 4lps in next ch sp, (dc in next dc, ch 1) repeat 15 times, repeat from * 1 (2, 3, 3) times, dc in next dc, work 4lps in next ch sp, (dc in next dc, ch 1) repeat 10 (4, 14, 8) times, dc in 3rd turning ch, turn.
Row 4: Ch 4, (dc in next dc, ch 1) repeat 8 (2, 12, 6) times, * dc in next dc, work 4lps in next ch sp, dc in next dc, ch 1, dc in next dc, work 4lps in next ch sp *, (dc in next dc, ch 1) repeat 13 times *, repeat from * to * 1 (2, 3, 3) times, dc in next dc, work 4lps in next ch sp, dc in next dc, ch 1, dc in next dc, work 4lps in next ch sp, dc in next dc, ch 1, dc in 3rd turning ch, turn.
Row 5: Work as row 3.
Rows 6, 7, and 8: Work as row 2.
Row 9: Ch 4, (dc in next dc, ch 1) repeat 9 times, * dc in next dc, work 4lps in next ch sp, (dc in next dc, ch 1) repeat 15 times, repeat from * 1 (1, 2, 2) times, dc in next dc, work 4lps in next ch sp, (dc in next dc, ch 1) repeat 2 (12, 6, 16) times, dc in 3rd turning ch, turn.
Row 10: Ch 4, (dc in next dc, ch 1) repeat 0 (10, 4, 14) times * dc in next dc, work 4lps in next ch sp, dc in next dc, ch 1, dc in next dc, work 4lps in next ch sp ** (dc in next dc, ch 1) repeat 13 times *, repeat from * to * 1 (1, 2, 2) times, then repeat from * to ** once more, (dc in next dc, ch 1) repeat 9 times, sc in 3rd turning ch, turn.
Row 11: Work as row 9.
Rows 12, 13, and 14: Work as row 2.
Repeat rows 3-12. Piece measures 9½ inches (24cm) ending with a WS row.

Row 25 (dec row): Ch 3, dc in next dc, (ch 1, dc in next dc) repeat 42 (52, 62, 72) times, ch 1, dc in next dc, dc in 3rd turning ch, turn.

Row 26: Ch 4, skip next dc, * dc in next dc, ch 1, * repeat 42 times, skip next dc, dc in turning ch, turn. 43 (53, 63, 73) sps.

Row 27: Ch 4, (dc in next dc, ch 1) repeat 16 times, dc in next dc, work 4lps in next ch sp, * (dc in next dc, ch 1) repeat 15 times, dc in next dc, work 4lps in next ch sp *, repeat from * 0 (1, 1, 2) times, (dc in next dc, ch 1) repeat 9 (3, 13, 7) times, dc in 3rd turning ch, turn.

Row 28: Ch 4, (dc in next dc, ch 1) repeat 7 (1, 11, 5) times, * dc in next dc, work 4lps in next ch sp, dc in next dc, ch 1, dc in next dc, work 4lps in next ch sp, (dc in next dc, ch 1) repeat 13 times *, repeat from * to * 0 (1, 1, 2) times, dc in next dc, work 4lps in next ch sp, dc in next dc, ch 1, dc in next dc, work 4lps in next ch sp, (dc in next dc, ch 1) repeat 16 times, dc in 3rd turning ch, turn.

Row 29: Work as row 27.

Row 30 (dec row): Ch 3, dc in next dc, (ch 1, dc in next dc) repeat 40 (50, 60, 70) times, ch 1, dc in next dc, dc in 3rd turning ch, turn.

Row 31: Ch 4, skip next dc, (dc in next dc, ch 1) repeat 40 (50, 60, 70) times, skip next dc, dc in turning ch, turn. 41 (51, 61, 71) sps.

Single crochet band

Row 1: Ch 1, (sc in next ch sp, sc in next dc) repeat to end, end with sc in 3rd turning ch, turn. 82 (102, 122, 142) sc.

Rows 2-8: Ch 1, sc in each sc to end, turn.

Row 9: Ch 1, sc in each sc to end, end with 2 sc into turning ch, turn. 83 (103, 123, 143) sc.

Crossed double crochet pattern and armhole shaping

Row 1: Ch 3, cdc to end of row, end with dc in turning ch, turn. 41 (51, 61, 71) cdc.

Row 2: Ch 1, sc in each sc to end, turn.

Rows 3-14: Work last 2 rows a total of 7 times.

Row 15: Ch 1, sl st in next 6 (6, 8, 8) sc, ch 3, cdc 35 (45, 53, 63) times, dc in next sc, leaving last 6 sts unworked, turn. 35 (45, 53, 63) cdc.

Row 16: Ch 1, sc in next sc, sc3tog, sc to last 4 sts, sc3tog, sc in next sc, sc in turning ch.

Row 17: Work as row 1. 33 (43, 51, 61) cdc.

Row 18: Work as row 16.

Rows 19-22: Work last 2 rows a total of 3 times. 27 (37, 45, 55) cdc.

Row 23: Work as row 1.

Row 24: Work as row 2.

Work last 2 rows a total of 8 (8, 9, 10) times. 27 (37, 45, 55) cdc.

Back right neck shaping

Row 38 (38, 40, 42): Ch 3, 6 (10, 13, 17) cdc, 1 dc in next dc, turn. Leave remaining sts unworked. 6 (10, 13, 17) cdc.

Row 39 (39, 41, 43): 1 sc in next sc, sc3tog, sc to end, turn.

Back left neck shaping

Row 38 (38, 40, 42): Skip next 30 sc, rejoin yarn, ch 3, cdc to end of row, end with dc in turning ch, turn. 6 cdc.

Row 39 (39, 41, 43): Ch 1, sc in each sc to the last 4 sts, sc3tog, sc in next sc, end with sc in turning ch, turn.

FRONT

Work as for back, completing row 24 of cdc pattern and armhole shaping.

Left neck shaping

Row 25: Ch 3, 10 (14, 17, 21) cdc, 1 dc in next dc, turn. Leave remaining sts unworked. 10 (14, 17, 21) cdc.

Row 26: Ch 1, sc in next sc, sc3tog, sc to end, turn.

Row 27: Ch 3, cdc to end of row, end with dc in turning ch, turn.

Rows 28-35: Work last 2 rows until there are 5 (9, 12, 16) cdc.

Row 36: Ch 1, sc in each sc to end, turn.

Row 37: Work as row 27.

Repeat last 2 rows until armhole measures same as back.

Right neck shaping

Row 25: Skip next 12 (16, 20, 24) sc, rejoin yarn, ch 3, cdc to end of row, end with dc in turning ch, turn.

Row 26: Ch 1, sc in each dc to the last 4 sts, sc3tog, sc in next dc, end with sc in turning ch, turn.

Row 27: Ch 3, cdc to end of row, end with dc in turning ch, turn. 10 (14, 17, 21) cdc.

Rows 28-35: Work last 2 rows until there are 5 (9, 12, 16) cdc.

Row 36: Ch 1, sc in each sc to end, turn.

Row 37: Work as row 27.

Repeat last 2 rows until armhole measures same as other side.

SLEEVES

Ch 51 (51, 55, 59).

Flower mesh pattern

Row 1 (RS): Dc in 5th ch from hook, * ch 1, skip 1 ch, dc in next ch, * repeat to end, turn. 23 (23, 25, 27) sps.

Row 2 (WS): Ch 4, * dc in next dc, ch 1, * repeat to end, dc in 3rd turning ch, turn.

Row 3: Ch 4, (dc in next dc, ch 1) repeat 2 (2, 3, 4) times, dc in next dc, work 4lps in next ch sp, (dc in next dc, ch 1) repeat 15 times, dc in next dc, work 4lps in next ch sp, (dc in next dc, ch 1) repeat 3 (3, 4, 5) times, dc in 3rd turning ch, turn.

Row 4: Ch 4 (dc in next dc, ch 1) repeat 1 (1, 2, 3) times, dc in next dc, work 4lps in next ch sp, dc in next dc, ch 1, dc in next dc, work 4lps in next ch sp, (dc in next dc, ch 1) repeat 13 times, dc in next dc, work 4lps in next ch sp, dc in next dc, ch 1, dc in next dc, work 4lps in next ch sp, (dc in next dc, ch 1) repeat 2 (2, 3, 4) times, dc in 3rd turning ch, turn.

Row 5: Work as row 3.

Rows 6, 7, and 8: Work as row 2.

Row 9: Ch 4, (dc in next dc, ch 1) repeat 10 (10, 11, 12) times, dc in next dc, work 4lps in next ch sp, (dc in next dc, ch 1) repeat 11 (11, 12, 13) times, dc in 3rd turning ch, turn.

Row 10: Ch 4, (dc in next dc, ch 1) repeat 9 (9, 10, 11) times, dc in next dc, work 4lps in next ch sp, dc in next dc, ch 1, dc in next dc, work 4lps in next ch sp, (dc in next dc, ch 1) repeat 10 (10, 11, 12) times, dc in 3rd turning ch, turn.

Row 11 (inc row): Ch 4, (1 dc, ch 1, 1 dc) in next dc, (ch 1, dc in next dc) repeat 10 (10, 11, 12) times, work 4lps in next ch sp, (dc in next dc, ch 1) repeat 10 (10, 11, 12) times, (1 dc, ch 1, 1 dc) in next dc, ch 1, dc in 3rd turning ch, turn. 25 (25, 27, 29) sps.

Rows 12, 13, and 14: Work as row 2.

Row 15 (inc row): Ch 4, (1 dc, ch 1, 1 dc) in next dc, (ch 1, dc in next dc) repeat 3 (3, 4, 5) times, work 4lps in next ch sp, (dc in next dc, ch 1) repeat 15 times, dc in next dc, work 4lps in next ch sp, (dc in next dc, ch 1) repeat 3 (3, 4, 5) times, (1 dc, ch 1, 1 dc), in next dc, ch 1, dc in 3rd turning ch, turn. 25 (25, 27, 29) sps.

Row 16: Ch 4, (dc in next dc, ch 1) repeat 3 (3, 4, 5) times, dc in next dc, work 4lps in next ch sp, dc in next dc, ch 1, dc in next dc, work 4lps in next ch sp, (dc in next dc, ch 1) repeat 13 times, dc in next dc, work 4lps in next ch sp, dc in next dc, ch 1, dc in next dc, work 4lps in next ch sp, (dc in next dc, ch 1) repeat 4 (4, 5, 6) times, dc in 3rd turning ch, turn.

Row 17: Ch 4, (dc in next dc, ch 1) repeat 4 (4, 5, 6) times, work 4lps in next ch sp, (dc in next dc, ch 1) repeat 15 times, dc in next dc, work 4lps in next ch sp, (dc in next dc, ch 1) repeat 4 (4, 5, 6) times, dc in 3rd turning ch, turn.

Rows 18 and 20: Work as row 2.

Row 19 (inc row): Ch 4, (1 dc, ch 1, 1 dc), in next dc, (ch 1, dc in next dc) repeat 25 (25, 27, 29) times, (1 dc, ch 1, 1 dc), in next dc, ch 1, dc in 3rd turning ch, turn. 29 (29, 31, 33) sps.

Row 21: Ch 4, (dc in next dc, ch 1), repeat 13 (13, 14, 15) times, dc in next dc, work 4lps in next ch sp, (dc in next dc, ch 1) repeat 14 (14, 15, 16) times, dc in 3rd turning ch, turn.

Row 22: Ch 4, (dc in next dc, ch 1) repeat 12 (12, 13, 14) times, dc in next dc, work 4lps in next ch sp, dc in next dc, ch 1, dc in next dc, work 4lps in next ch sp, (dc in next dc, ch 1), repeat 13 (13, 14, 15) times, dc in 3rd turning ch, turn.

Row 23 (inc row): Ch 4, (1 dc, ch 1, 1 dc) in next dc, (ch 1, dc in next dc) repeat 13 (13, 14, 15) times, work 4lps in next ch sp, (dc in next dc, ch 1) repeat 13 (13, 14, 15) times, (1 dc, ch 1, 1 dc) in next dc, ch 1, dc in 3rd turning ch, turn. 31 (31, 33, 35) sps.

Rows 24, 25, and 26: Work as row 2.

Row 27 (inc row): Ch 4, (1 dc, ch 1, 1 dc) in next dc, (ch 1, dc in next dc) repeat 6 (6, 7, 8) times, work 4lps in next ch sp, (dc in next dc, ch 1)

repeat 15 times, dc in next dc, work 4lps in next ch sp, (dc in next dc, ch 1) repeat 6 (6, 7, 8) times, (1 dc, ch 1, 1 dc) in next dc, ch 1, dc in 3rd turning ch, turn. 33 (33, 35, 37) sps.

Row 28: Ch 4, (dc in next dc, ch 1) repeat 6 (6, 7, 8) times, dc in next dc, work 4lps in next ch sp, dc in next dc, ch 1, dc in next dc, work 4lps in next ch sp, (dc in next dc, ch 1), repeat 13 times, dc in next dc, work 4lps in next ch sp, dc in next dc, ch 1, dc in next dc, work 4lps in next ch sp, (dc in next dc, ch 1) repeat 7 (7, 8, 9) times, dc in 3rd turning ch, turn.

Row 29: Ch 4, (dc in next dc, ch 1) repeat 7 times, work 4lps in next ch sp, (dc in next dc, ch 1) repeat 15 times, dc in next dc, work 4lps in next ch sp, (dc in next dc, ch 1) repeat 8 (8, 9, 10) times, dc in 3rd turning ch, turn.

Rows 30 and 31: Work as row 2. 33 (33, 35, 57) sps.

Single crochet band

Row 1: Ch 1, (sc in next ch sp, sc in next dc) repeat to end, end with sc in 3rd turning ch, turn. 66 (66, 70, 74) sc.

Row 2-8: Ch 1, sc in each sc to end, turn.

Row 9: Ch 1, sc in each sc to end, end with 2 sc into turning ch, turn. 67 (67, 71, 75) sc.

Crossed double crochet pattern

Row 1: Ch 3, cdc to end of row, end with dc in turning ch, turn. 33 (33, 35, 37) cdc.

Row 2: Ch 1, sc in each sc to end, turn.

Work rows 1 and 2 a total of 7 (7, 8, 9) times.

Cap shaping

Row 1: Ch 1, sl st in next 6 (6, 8, 10) sc, ch 3, cdc 27 times, dc in next sc, leaving last 6 (6, 8, 10) sts unworked, turn. 27 cdc.

Row 2: Ch 1, sc in next sc, sc3tog, sc to last 4 sts, sc3tog, sc in next sc, sc in turning ch.

Row 3: Ch 3, cdc to end of row, end with dc in turning ch, turn. 25 cdc.

Row 4: Work as row 2.

Work last 2 rows a total of 3 times. 19 cdc.

FINISHING

Block the crocheted pieces lightly (see page 137).
With yarn and tapestry needle, sew shoulder seams.
Position sleeves in armhole opening, sew in place.
Sew sleeve and side seams. Weave in all loose ends.

Edgings

Sc 1 row around neck opening, lower edge of sleeve, and lower edge of tunic.

This gorgeous lilac swing cardigan is oh-so-pretty, with its decorative yoke and unusual floral tie fastenings. Instead of using ribbon, the designer has torn up strips of floral fabric and woven these through the double crochet rows, giving a contemporary twist and a unique feel to this lovely piece. This is a great way to reinvent favorite dresses or vintage silk scarves that have seen better days—don't worry if the fabric frays; it will add to the charm.

"Millie" Cardigan   Alicia Paulson

MATERIALS
12 (14, 15, 16) balls Debbie Bliss Cashmerino Aran (55% merino wool, 33% microfiber, 12% cashmere, approx. 1¾ oz/50g, 98 yards/90m), shade 012 Dusky Pink
Size 4mm (F/5) crochet hook (see page 120)
Size 4.25mm (G/6) crochet hook (see page 120)
Three strips of fabric, each approximately 1¼ yards (1.2m) long and ⅝ inch (1.5cm) wide
Tapestry needle
Stitch marker

MEASUREMENTS
To fit four sizes: S (M, L, XL).
Bust measurement: 38 (40, 44, 48) inches (97 [102, 112, 122]cm).
Length: 17 (17, 17½, 17½) inches (43 [43, 44, 44]cm).
Sleeve length: 17 (17, 17½, 17½) inches (43 [43, 44, 44]cm).

NOTE
Instructions for larger sizes are given in parentheses. Where there is only one figure, it applies to all sizes.

GAUGE
16 sts and 19 rows to 4 inches (10cm) over body pattern stitch, using size 4.25mm (G/6) crochet hook or the size required to obtain the correct gauge.

ABBREVIATIONS
See page 120.

SPECIAL ABBREVIATIONS
RF: Right front.
LF: Left front.
inc: Increase.

YOKE
Using smaller hook, ch 71.
Row 1 (RS): Dc in 4th ch from hook, dc in each ch across to end; turn. 68 sts.
Row 2: Ch 3 (counts as first dc), (dc in next dc, 2 dc in next dc, dc in next dc) 22 times, dc in next dc; turn. 90 sts.
Row 3: Ch 3, dc in each dc across to end; turn. 90 sts.
Row 4: Ch 3, (1 dc in next dc, 2 dc in next dc, dc in next 2 dc) 22 times, dc in last dc; turn. 112sts.
Row 5: Repeat row 3. 112 sts.
Row 6: Ch 3, (dc in next 2 dc, 2 dc in next dc, dc in next 2 dc) 22 times, dc in next dc; turn. 134 sts.
Row 7: Repeat row 3. 134 sts.
Row 8: Ch 3, (dc in next 3 dc, 2 dc in next dc, dc in next 2 dc) 22 times, dc in next dc; turn. 156 sts.
Row 9: Repeat row 3. 156 sts.

Divide yoke for sizes S and M
Row 10: Ch 3, (dc in next 3 dc, 2 dc in next dc, dc in next 3 dc) 22 times. 178 sts.
Row 11: Repeat row 3. 178 sts.

Divide yoke for sizes L and XL
For left front: Place marker at st 22 (22, 26, 26) from edge.
For left sleeve: Place marker at st 34 (34, 38, 38) from edge of LF (in other words, start counting from last st of LF, or at st 23 from edge).

For back: Place marker at st 44 (44, 52, 52) from edge of left sleeve.
For right sleeve: Place marker at st 34 (34, 38, 38) counted from edge of back piece.
For right front: You should have 22 (22, 26, 26) sts (including first ch-3, which counted as first sc).

LEFT FRONT

Row 1: With larger hook, ch 1, skip first dc, 2 sc in next dc, (skip next dc, 2 sc in next dc) 10 (10, 12, 12) times more, sc in last st (inc made); turn. 23 (23, 27, 27) sts.

Row 2: Ch 1, 2 sc in 1st sc (inc made), 2 sc in next sc, (skip next sc, 2 sc in next sc) 10 (10, 12, 12) times; turn. 24 (24, 28, 28 sts.
Repeat rows 1 and 2 fourteen (16, 16, 20) more times. 38 (40, 44, 48) sts.
Work straight for 46 (46, 48, 48) rows more until LF measures 13 (13½, 14, 14½) inches (33 [34, 36, 37]cm) from bottom of yoke (not neckline).

LEFT SLEEVE

Row 1: With larger hook, attach yarn with sl st in next st over from edge of LF. Ch 1, sc in same sc as ch-1, 2 sc in next sc (inc made), (skip next sc, 2 sc in next sc) 16 (16, 18, 18) times, sc again in last sc (inc made); turn. [36 (36, 40, 40) sts].

Row 2: Ch 1, 2 sc in first sc, 2 sc in next sc, (skip next sc, 2 sc in next sc) 17 (17, 19, 19) times, 2 sc in last sc; turn. 38 (38, 42, 42) sts.
Repeat rows 1 and 2 fourteen (16, 16, 20) more times. 66 (70, 74, 82) sts.
Work straight for 46 (46, 48, 48) more rows until sleeve measures 13 (13½, 14, 14½) inches (33 [34, 36, 37]cm) from bottom of yoke (not neckline).

BACK

Row 1: Using larger hook, attach yarn with sl st in next st over from edge of left sleeve. Ch 1, sc in same sc as ch-1, 2 sc in next sc (inc made), (skip next sc, 2 sc in next sc) 21 (21, 25, 25) times, sc again in last sc (inc made); turn. 46 (46, 54, 54) sts.

Row 2: Ch 1, 2 sc in first sc, 2 sc in next sc, (skip next sc, 2 sc in next sc) 22 (22, 26, 26) times, 2 sc in last sc; turn. 48 (48, 56, 56) sts.
Repeat rows 1 and 2 fourteen (16, 16, 20) more times. 76 (80, 88, 96) sts.
Work straight for 46 (46, 48, 48) more rows more until back measures 13 (13½, 14, 14½) inches (33 [34, 36, 37]cm) from bottom of yoke (not neckline).

RIGHT SLEEVE

Row 1: Using larger hook, attach yarn with sl st in next st over from edge of back. Work as for left sleeve, reversing shaping.

RIGHT FRONT

Row 1: Using larger hook, attach yarn with sl st in next st over from edge of right sleeve. Work as for left front, reversing shaping.

FINISHING

Sew sleeves to fronts and back. Sew up sides, and then underarms. With RS facing, join yarn at left side seam. Sc in bottom loop of each sc across back and RF. Make 3 sc in last stitch of RF to turn corner. Sc evenly up RF and yoke, and in each loop of dc around neck opening. Make 3 sc in last stitch of neck to turn corner down yoke. Sc down edge of yoke and LF, making 3 sc around corner of LF, and continue across bottom of LF. Join with sl st into first sc. Fasten off.

Darn in all ends and press lightly (see page 137).
Weave fabric strips through dc around yoke where comfortable, and tie in a bow to close.

Besides making a fashion statement, this retro kerchief is a great way to keep the wind at bay or keep your head warm when it's chilly outside. The body of the headscarf is made in zigzag forget-me-knot stitch with a pretty picot edging. The ribbon woven through the eyelets can be of either a matching or a contrasting color.

Rickrack Kerchief

Juju Vail

MATERIALS

Debbie Bliss Baby Cashmerino (worsted, 55% merino wool, 33% microfiber, 12% Cashmere, approx. 1¾ oz/50g, 136¾ yards/125m) in the following shades and quantities:
2 balls shade 103 Peach (yarn A)
1 ball shade 11 Brown (yarn B)
Size 3mm (C/2½) crochet hook (see page 120)
Tapestry needle
¾ yard (70cm) mint green velvet ribbon, ½ inch (1cm) wide
Sewing needle and thread to match ribbon color

MEASUREMENTS

Length from edge of headband to tip of triangle: 16 inches (40cm).
Width across base of triangle: 22 inches (57cm).
Width including tie: 32 inches (82cm).

GAUGE

Using size 3mm (C/2½) hook, or size to obtain the correct gauge, make a swatch of rickrack stitch, as follows. Make a base chain of 21 plus 2 turning ch. Follow instructions for rickrack stitch for 14 rows, making every 4th row in an alternate color. This should make a swatch of 4 x 4 inches (10 x 10cm).

ABBREVIATIONS

See page 120.

RICKRACK STITCH

Work stitch over a number of chain divisible by 3, plus 2 turning chain.

Row 1: Into 4th chain from hook work (1 dc, ch 2, 1 sc), * skip next ch-2, (1 dc, ch 2, 1 sc) into next ch, rep from * to end. Turn.

Row 2: Ch 3, (1 dc, ch 2, 1 sc) into first ch-2 space, * (1 dc, ch 2, 1 sc) into next ch-2 space, rep from * to end. Turn.

The last row is repeated throughout to form the pattern. Every 4th row is worked in an alternate color.

KERCHIEF RIBBON BAND

Using yarn A, ch 111 plus 2 turning chain.

Row 1: Switch to yarn B. Sc 1 row, starting with 3rd ch from hook.

Row 2: Ch 2, repeat row 1.

Row 3 (eyelet row): * 2 hdc, ch 1 skip next st *. Repeat 35 times, 3 hdc, turn.

Rows 4 and 5: Repeat row 2.

RICKRACK FABRIC AND DECREASES

Row 1 (rickrack stitch): Using yarn A, work first row of rickrack stitch into top loops of 110 sts from previous row (skip final loop).

For rows 1, 2 and 3 use yarn A and for row 4 use yarn B. Cut and rejoin the yarn for each color change.

Row 2: Continue in rickrack stitch over the 110 sts, making decreases (see instructions below) on rows 2 and 3 of yarn A for the first 27 rows. Therefore, these decreases will appear on the following rows: 2, 3, 6, 7, 10, 11, 14, 15, 18, 19, 22, 23, 26 and 27.

After row 27, decrease on every row for the next 5¾ repeats of the pattern, ending with 3 rows of yarn A. This will make a total of 50 rows. Pull yarn through final loop.

To make a decrease: Ch 3, skip the first ch-2 space and work into the second ch-2 space. Continue to end of row as usual.

TIE EXTENSION

Row 1: Using yarn B, make 6 sc into the edge stitches of the ribbon band.

Row 2: Ch 2, 6 sc, turn.

Work 20 rows and then decrease 1 st on each side until 1 st remains (forming a point). Cut yarn and pull through st.

Repeat for other end of tie.

EDGE STITCH

Beginning with top left edge of ribbon band and using yarn A, work sc around the edge of ribbon band.

Continue around band point, working 3 sc into the top point of band to turn the corner.

Sc until you reach the rickrack stitch and then work in picot-edge stitch as follows.

Picot-edge stitch

Row 1: 3 sc into yarn A edge loop, 3 sc into yarn B edge loop. Repeat until you reach the tip. 26 sc. Make 3 sc into loop at tip of scarf and then continue down other side as before. Stop at the end of the rickrack fabric, turn.

Row 2: * Ch 5, sl st into 2nd chain from hook, ch 2, sc into 3rd sc loop of previous row. * Continue making picot edging all around rickrack fabric of kerchief.

Cut yarn and pull through last stitch to fasten off.

Using yarn A, go back to unfinished edge of yarn B ribbon band and work in sl st around outer edge as for the first tie edge.

FINISHING

Darn all yarn ends into the crochet fabric securely and trim. Thread ribbon through the holes in the band and secure with a few stitches, using sewing needle and thread, on the wrong side of both ends.

Sweet little crochet rosettes are fashioned into a short-sleeved waist-length shrug, named for favorite World War II pinup girl Betty Grable. Made from delicious Blue Sky Alpacas sportweight yarn in soft nickel gray, the motifs can be worked one at a time and joined into the finished garment as you go, so seaming is kept to a minimum. Fasten with a vintage button or brooch.

"Betty" Shrug   Kristeen Griffin-Grimes

MATERIALS

Blue Sky Alpacas Sportweight (100% baby alpaca, approx. 1¾ oz/50g, 109⅜ yards/100m) in the following shades and quantities:

  Size S-M: 7 balls shade 524 Nickel

  Sizes L and XL: 8 balls, as above

Size S-M: Size 3.75mm (F/5) crochet hook (see page 120)

Sizes L and XL: Size 4.25mm (G/6) crochet hook (see page 120)

Stitch marker

MEASUREMENTS

To fit three sizes: S-M, L, and XL.

Back length: 16 (17½, 18) inches (41 [44, 46]cm), measured from top to point of bottom motif.

Sleeve length at underarm: 6½ (7, 8) inches (16 [18, 20]cm).

Width at hem: 39 (44, 47½) inches (99 [112, 120]cm).

Garment is constructed so that front edges hang lower than back hem.

NOTE

Instructions for larger sizes are given in parentheses. Where there is only one figure, it applies to all sizes.

GAUGE

Motif size: 5½ x 5½ inches (14 x 14cm) using size 3.75mm (F/5) hook; 6 x 6 inches (15.5 x 15.5cm with size 4.25mm (G/6) hook. Change size if necessary to obtain the correct gauge.

ABBREVIATIONS

See page 120.

SPECIAL ABBREVIATIONS

M + number: Motif with number referring to the diagram on page 39.

dc2tog—decrease by working 2 dc tog: Work 1 dc leaving 2 loops remaining on hook, work 2nd dc into same st, until there are 3 loops remaining, then complete both sts as 1 st, by yo and pulling yarn through all 3 loops on hook.

dc3tog cl—dc3tog cluster: Work 1 dc leaving 2 loops on hook, work 2nd dc into same st until 3 loops remain, work 3rd dc until 4 loops remain, then yo, pull yarn through 2 loops, yo, pull yarn through remaining 3 loops.

dc4tog cl—dc4tog cluster: Work 1 dc leaving 2 loops on hook, work 2nd dc into same st until 3 loops remain, work 3rd dc until 4 loops remain, work 4th dc until 5 loops remain then yo, pull yarn through 2 loops (4 loops remain), yo, pull yarn through remaining 4 loops.

MOTIFS

Motif 1

Round 1: Form circle, into which to begin the motif, as follows: Holding short tail of yarn taut, wrap yarn around index finger twice. Keeping circle intact and continuing to hold short tail in place, insert crochet hook into opening in circle and draw through loop, ch 3 (counts as 1 dc). Place 15 more dc in the ring (16 total dc). Join the last dc with a sl st to 3rd ch of first ch-3. As you work, tighten up opening in circle until, after all sts are placed for first round, the circle is completely closed.

Round 2: Ch 4 (counts as 1 dc + ch-1), (1 dc, ch 1) in each of next 15 dc in ring. Join with sl st to 4th ch in first ch-4.

Round 3: Ch 3, dc2tog into same space as ch-3 (counts as 1 cluster), then ch 2, (dc3tog, ch 2) into 15 remaining ch-1 spaces from round 2, ending last cluster with dc3tog, then dc into top of first dc2tog. 16 cluster sts.

Round 4: Ch 1, sc into top of first dc2tog from round 3 (same spot where you placed joining dc at end of round 3). * Ch 5, sc into ch-2 space from round 3, repeat from * until last ch-2 space. Ch 2, then dc into sc at beginning of round.

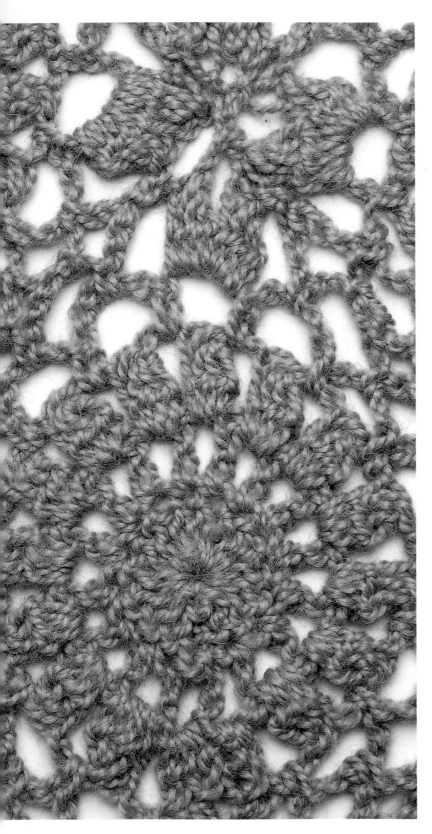

Round 5: Ch 3, then (dc3tog, ch 3, dc4tog) into the space in last ch loop from round 4 (first corner cluster made). *(Ch 5, sc into next ch-5 loop) 3 times, ch 5, place (dc4tog cl, ch 3, dc4tog cl) into the next ch-5 loop from round 4 (2nd corner cluster made). Continue around motif repeating from * making 3rd corner cluster and ending with ch 5 in first dc3tog at beginning of round. Fasten off.

Motif 2

After completing motif 1, work motif 2 to the end of round 4 and, referring to the chart, join them in this manner: learn to recognize where the corners of the motifs will fall to aid in joining motifs.

Sizes S–M and L: On M2 begin round 5, work up to 3rd dc4tog cluster group (3rd corner) and join to M1: ** make 1 dc4tog cl, ch 1, sl st into ch-3 space between the two dc4tog cl on M1, ch 1, complete 2nd dc4tog cl on M2 **, * ch 2, sl st into ch-5 space on M1, ch 2, sl st into ch-5 space on M2, repeating from * until you reach the next corner. Repeat from ** to **, then ch 5 and complete remaining side as directed in round 5.

Size XL: On M2 begin round 5, work up to 3rd dc4tog cluster group (3rd corner) and join to M1: ** make 1 dc4tog cl, ch 2, sl st into ch-3 space between the two dc4tog cl on M1, ch 2, complete 2nd dc4tog cl on M2 **, * ch 3, sl st into ch-5 space on M1, ch 3, sl st into ch-5 space on M2, repeating from * until you reach the next corner. Repeat from ** to **, then ch 5 and complete remaining side as directed in round 5.

Join M3 to M1 in the same manner.

Join M4 to M1/2/3: This is the first of the motifs joined to the others on only 2 sides, leaving a rounded edge (these motifs are denoted by a * on the chart).

Begin round 5 as directed above for M1, making only first cluster in M4, then ch 1, sl st into the ch-3 space between corner clusters on M2, continue to join sides of M4 and M2 as directed above until the next corner is reached, continuing in established pattern. Remember to sl st all the corner clusters together at the point where all motifs meet (into the ch-3 between the sc4tog cl), then continue in established joining pattern up the other side joining M4 to M3. End with ch 5 after 3rd corner is joined and sl st to ch-5 of round 4 on M4.

You will now have completed the first module of 4 motifs; the intersection where the 4 corners meet is the center-back line of the garment. Now continue to construct and join motifs in the order given, remembering to join the starred motifs to leave a rounded edge as directed above in joining M4. The starred motifs along the neckline will have the rounded edges at the top and the lower ones will have the rounded edges at the bottom.

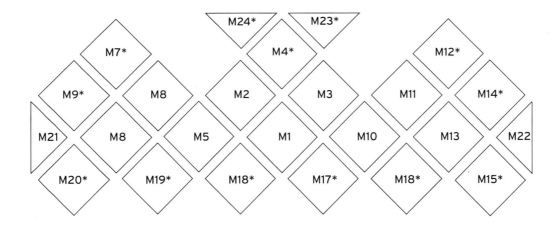

Shrug body

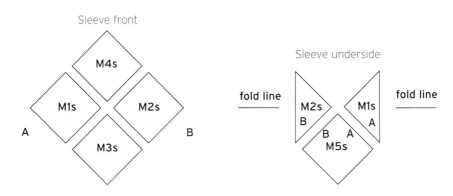

Sleeve front

Sleeve underside

Once you have completed joining the motifs to M20, construct 2 half motifs (M21 and M22) to complete the right and left fronts. These are made by working back and forth instead of in rounds.

Motif 21

Row 1: Start motif as usual, placing only 10 dc in yarn ring. Turn.

Row 2: Work in established pattern, placing only 9 (dc, ch 1), ending with 1 dc in last dc from first round. Turn.

Row 3: Work in pattern, placing only 9 (dc3tog cluster, ch 2), end with 1 dc3tog cluster in dc from previous round. Turn.

Row 4: Ch 5, sc in next ch-2 space from previous round, repeat to end placing last sc in top of last dc3tog cluster from round 3. Leave yarn attached and attach to right and left fronts as follows.

Join M21 to M9 and M20.

Sizes S–M and L: Ch 5, sl st to ch-3 between 2 dc4tog clusters at left point of M20, ch 1, place 1 dc4tog cluster in first ch-5 loop on M21, ch 2, (sl st into next ch-5 loop on M20; ch 2, sl st into the next ch-5 loop on

M21), repeat this twice more, ch 2, sl st into the last ch-5 loop before 4-dc cluster corner on M20, ch 2, place 1 dc4tog cluster in next ch-5 loop on M21, ch 1, sl st into point where M20, M8 and M9 join (this will be the ch-3 between dc4tog clusters in each of the corners of these motifs), ch 1, place the second sc4tog cluster into the same ch-5 loop on M21 (2 clusters placed in same loop), then (ch 2, sl st into next ch-5 loop on M9, ch 2, sl st into next ch-5 loop on M21), repeat this twice more. Ch 2, sl st into last ch-5 loop before corner cluster on M9, ch 2, place 1 dc4tog cluster in last ch-5 loop on M21, ch 1, sl st into ch-3 between 2 dc4tog clusters on M9, ch 5, sl sl st to last ch-5 loop from round 4 on M21. Fasten off.

Size XL: Ch 5, sl st to ch-3 between 2 dc4tog clusters at left point of M20, ch 2, place 1 dc4tog cluster in first ch-5 loop on M21, ch 3, (sl st into next ch-5 loop on M20; ch 3, sl st into the next ch-5 loop on M21), repeat this twice more, ch 3, sl st into last ch-5 loop before 4-dc cluster corner on M20, ch 3, place 1 dc4tog cluster in next ch-5 loop on M21, ch 2, sl st into point where M20, M8 and M9 join (this will be the ch-3 between dc4tog clusters in each of the corners of these motifs, ch 2, place the second sc4tog cluster into the same ch-5 loop on M21 (2 clusters placed in same loop), then (ch 3, sl st into next ch-5 loop on M9, ch 3, sl st into next ch-5 loop on M21), repeat this twice more. Ch 2, sl st into last ch-5 loop before corner cluster on M9, ch 3, place 1 dc4tog cluster in last ch-5 loop on M21, ch 2, sl st into ch-3 between 2 dc4tog clusters on M9, ch 5, sl st to last ch-5 loop from round 4 on M21. Fasten off.

Join M22 in the same way, starting by joining to M14, then to M15.

Complete the neckline to prepare for joining sleeves.
Before joining the sleeves and completing top edging, mark the following on motifs:
1 The point where right corner of M7 meets top corner of M9—for button placement (optional).
2 The point opposite that where corner of M12 joins M14—for button loop (optional).
3 Two places on M4: the 2nd ch-5 loop above both the left and right corner—for joining gusset M23 and M24.
4 The same point as in 3 above, on right side of M7 and left side of M12—for aiding in sleeve placement.

GUSSETS

Make 2 small gussets (M23 and M24) as follows:
Make and join M24 to M4.
Row 1: Begin motif in pattern, placing only 6 dc in yarn ring, not tightening up ring entirely, for use in row 5, turn.
Row 2: Ch 4 (counts as 1 dc + ch-1), place 4 more (1 dc, ch-1) in next 4 dc from round 1; dc in last dc, turn.
Row 3: Repeat round 3 of pattern, placing 5 clusters (1 cluster + ch-2) in each of the ch-1 spaces from round 2, turn.
Row 4: * Ch 5, sc into top ch-2 space from row 3, repeat from * to end, ending with sl st last ch-5 to last dc3tog cluster.
Row 5: Work around the left side, across the bottom point and up the right side of the gusset.
Sizes S-M and L: Ch 5, attach with sl st to sc from row 2; ch 5, ** place 1 dc3tog cluster in yarn ring, ch 1, sl st into corner cluster where M2 and M4 join, ch 1, place 1 dc3tog cluster in yarn ring, tighten up ring **. Continue joining M24 to M4. Ch 2, sl st to next ch-5 on M4, ch 2, sl st to dc from row 2 of M24; ch 2, sl st to next ch-5 on M4 (marked), ch 2, sl st to first ch-3 in row 3 of M24. Fasten off.
Size XL: Ch 5, attach with sl st to sc from row 2; ch 5, ** place 1 dc3tog cluster in yarn ring, ch 2, sl st into corner cluster where M2 and M4 join, ch 2, place 1 dc3tog cluster in yarn ring, tighten up ring **. Continue joining M24 to M4. Ch 3, sl st to next ch-5 on M4, ch3, sl st to dc from row 2 of M24; ch 3, sl st to next ch-5 on M4 (marked), ch 3, sl st to first ch-3 in row 3 of M24. Fasten off.

Make and join M23 to M4.
Rows 1-4: Complete M23 as rows 1-4 of M24.
Row 5: Work around the left side joining M23 to M4, across the bottom point, joining to M3 at its top point, then working up the right side preparing the edge for joining to the sleeve.
Sizes S-M and L: Ch 2, sl st to marked ch-5 (2nd ch-5 above corner dc4tog cluster on M4), ch 2, sl st to dc from row 2 of M23; ch 2, sl st into next ch-5 on M4, then ch-2 and repeat from ** to ** on row 5 above. Now working without joining to any motifs, ch 5, sl st into dc from row 2 on M23, ch 5, sl st to the first ch-3 in row 3 of M23. Keep yarn attached for use later (secure by safety-pinning st closed).
Size XL: Ch 3, sl st to marked ch-5 (2nd ch-5 above corner dc4tog cluster on M4), ch 3, sl st to dc from row 2 of M23; ch 3, sl st into next ch-5 on M4, then ch-3 and repeat from ** to ** on row 5 above. Now working without joining to any motifs, ch 5, sl st into dc from row 2 on M23, ch 5, sl st to first ch-3 in row 3 of M23. Keep yarn attached for use later (secure by safety-pinning st closed).

SLEEVES (Make 2)

Right sleeve: Complete M1s as M1 of garment body. Complete M2s as M1s, working row 5 and joining M1s and M2s at one corner, completing an entire row 5 around M2s. M3 and M4 will now be inserted into the two spaces to form the main sleeve: working in the same manner as M4 of body, join M3s and then M4s, making sure to leave two sides of each unworked to form the top and hem of sleeve. (Leave yarn attached.) Complete M5s to row 4 of pattern, then, using row 5, join right edge to M1s (marked as A on chart), work into corners of M1s and M2s with dc4tog clusters as pattern, continue to finish joining to M2s (marked as B on chart), working in row 5 as written, making sure to leave 2 sides unworked for rounded lower edge of sleeve.
Once sleeves are completed, on M5s mark the 2nd ch-5 above where round 5 begins and ends on each.

Insert sleeves

For ease in placing sleeve, temporarily safety-pin corners of junction of M3, M10 and M11 on garment body to junction of M2s, M1s and M4s on sleeve.

Join right sleeve

Sizes S-M and L: Picking up yarn held back when joining M23 to garment and working from the underside, ch 5, sl st to marked ch-5 on M5s, ch 2, sl st to last ch-5 from row 5 of M23, ch 2, sl st to next ch-5 in M23, ch 2, sl st into center of sc4tog cluster where M5s and M1s join, ch 2, sl st into spot where M3, M4 and M23 join, ch 2, sl st into next ch-5 in M1s.

Size XL: Picking up yarn held back when joining M23 to garment and working from the underside, ch 5, sl st to marked ch-5 on M5s, ch 3, sl st to last ch-5 from row 5 of M23, ch 3, sl st to next ch-5 in M23, ch3, sl st into center of sc4tog cluster where M5s and M1s join, ch 3, sl st into spot where M3, M4 and M23 join, ch 3, sl st into next ch-5 in M1s.

Continue in this way across underarm, working into the point where M1s, M2s and M4s (and M1, M3 and M11 join) as if it were a ch-5. Continue around, joining sleeve to body, working up the side of M2s, treating the join of M2s and M5s, and M11 and M12, as a point to sl st into. Finish with established pattern at marked spot on M12. Leave yarn attached—complete top edge from this point after left sleeve is inserted.

Join left sleeve

Attach yarn to spot marked on left top of M5s, ch 2, sl st to spot marked on M7, then continue as described for right sleeve to join sleeve to body, working around underarm, ending by joining M5s to M23, completing join at spot marked on right side of M5s. Fasten off.

Complete top edge

Taking up yarn held from joining right sleeve, mark that spot (this denotes beginning and end of top edge section).
Ch 5, sl st in the top of next ch-5 loop, working from right to left across top edge and sleeve tops until marker on left edge of M7, * sl st in that loop, ch 2, dc into next ch. * Turn. Ch 5, sl st into next ch-5 loop, working back across entire top edge over beginning point (move marker to current row), to right front edge marker on M12, repeat from * to *. Work back to beginning point (2 rows completed). Try on garment to determine how many more edging rows are needed. Garment as shown has 6 rows. If more rows are needed, work the next 2 rows (or more) with ch-4 instead of ch-5, ending with last 2 rows using ch-3. Work to beginning marker, fasten off yarn and weave in all ends.

FINISHING
Button and button loop

If desired, sew a vintage button on the left side at spot marked. On right side, attach yarn securely, make a ch with enough sts to slide securely over button; work back over ch with sc sts, fasten and secure yarn.

Block the garment lightly (see page 137).

This gorgeous hat and scarf set, made in rich berry-colored cashmere worked in a textured bobble stitch with contrasting edging, is the ultimate in luxury. The super-soft yarn feels wonderful against the skin and will keep you feeling cozy and looking chic on the coldest of winter days.

"Lula" Scarf and Cloche Hat

Juju Vail

MATERIALS

For scarf: 3 balls Jade Sapphire 8-ply (Aran [worsted] weight) Cashmere (100% Mongolian cashmere, approx. 1⁹⁄₁₀ oz/55g, 109³⁄₈ yards/100m), shade 024 Plum Rose (yarn A)

One ball Jade Sapphire 6-ply (DK) Cashmere (100% Mongolian cashmere, approx. 1⁹⁄₁₀ oz/55g, 109³⁄₈ yards/100m), shade 023 Pebble Beach (yarn B)

For cloche hat: 3 balls Jade Sapphire 8-ply, shade 024 Plum Rose, as above

For scarf and hat: Sizes 4.5mm (G/7) and 3mm (C/2½) crochet hooks Tapestry needle

MEASUREMENTS

Scarf length: 61 inches (154cm); bobble end sections (x 2): 15 inches (38cm); middle sections (x 2): 12 inches (30cm) in yarn A and 3½ inches (9cm) in yarn B.

Scarf width: 6½ inches (16cm).

Hat diameter at widest part of brim: 12½ inches (32cm).

GAUGE

8 rows x 5 clusters = 4 x 4 inches (10 x 10cm) using size 4.5mm (G/7) hook or the size required to obtain the correct gauge.

ABBREVIATIONS

See page 120.

SPECIAL ABBREVIATIONS

cl—cluster: 1 hdc, 1 dc, 1 hdc all in the same sp.
mb—make bobble: Take yarn over hook, insert hook into ch, loop or sp, yarn over hook and draw through a loop (3 loops on hook), yarn over hook and draw through 2 loops. Repeat this 5 times (6 loops on hook), yarn over hook and draw through all 6 loops.

SCARF

Bobble ends

Using yarn A and larger hook, begin scarf with 8 ch, turn.
Sc in each st to end. Turn.
Row 1: Ch 1, mb, 2 sc, mb, 2 sc, mb. Turn.
Row 2: Ch 1, 7 sc, 3 sc in last st on row. Turn.
Row 3: Ch 1, mb, 2 sc, mb, 2 sc, mb, 2 sc, mb. Turn.
Row 4: Ch 1, 3 sc in first st, 10 sc. Turn.
Row 5: Ch 1, * mb, 2 sc* 5 times. Turn.
Row 6: Ch 1, 13 sc, 3 sc in last st. Turn.
Row 7: Ch 1, * mb, 2 sc* 6 times. Turn.
Row 8: Ch 1, 3 sc in first st, 16 sc. Turn.
Row 9: Ch 1, * mb, 2 sc* 7 times. Turn.
Row 10: Ch 1, 19 sc, 3 sc in last st. Turn.
Row 11: Ch 1, * mb, 2 sc* 8 times. Turn.
Row 12: Ch 1, 21 sc. Turn.
Row 13: Ch 1, * 2 sc, mb * 8 times. Turn.
Even rows 14, 16, 18, 20, 22, 24, 26, and 28: Repeat row 12.
Rows 15, 19, 23, and 27: Repeat row 11.
Rows 17, 21, and 25: Repeat row 13.

Neck middle

Change to Yarn B.
Row 1: Ch 2, hdc in next loop, * skip 2 loops, 1 cl in 3rd loop *, repeat 5 more times. Skip 1 loop, 2 hdc in last loop. Turn.
Row 2: Ch 2, 1 cl in each of the next 7 sps, 2 hdc into last loop of row. Turn.
Rows 3–8: Repeat last row, ending each row with a half cluster (2 hdc) into the last sp.

Change to yarn A and repeat row 2 twenty-nine times. Cut yarn and pull through loop to fasten off.

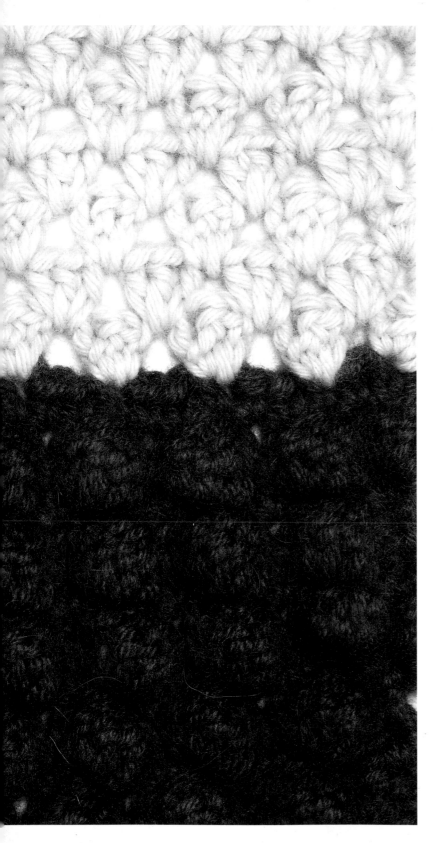

Repeat instructions from the beginning to make the other side of the scarf. Darn in ends and trim. Graft scarf middle backs together so that bobbles are both on the same side (see page 137).

Contrasting trim
Using smaller hook, begin crochet trim in yarn B at the end of a bobble section (where yarn B clusters begin).
Work 3 sc into the loop at the end of every other row. When you come to the beginning of the other side bobbles, cut yarn and pull through last stitch. Darn in end. Repeat for the other edge of scarf.

CLOCHE HAT
The hat is worked in the round, so the work is not turned between rows. Using larger hook, ch 3, join with sl st to form a ring.
Round 1: Ch 2, 1 dc, 1 hdc into center of ring, work 3 cl into ring, join with sl st to beginning 3rd chain (12 sts into center of ring).
Round 2: Ch 2, 1 dc, 1 hdc into the same sp as ch-2, * skip 3 loops from previous row and work 1 cl between next stitches * (clusters are worked between groups of clusters, every 3 sts). Repeat from * twice, skip 3 sts and work final cl in same sp as first cl, join with sl st to beginning ch-2 (24 sts or 8 cl).
Round 3: Ch 2, 1 dc, 1 hdc into same sp as ch-2. * 2 cl between next pair of clusters, 1 cl between next pair of cl *. Repeat 2 more times, 1 cl in last sp. Sl st to beginning ch-2 (36 sts or 12 cl).
Round 4: Ch 2, 1 dc, 1 hdc into same sp as ch-2. * 1 cl between next cl, 1 cl between pair of cl, 2 cl between next cl *. Repeat from * twice. 1 cl between cl, 1 cl between cl, 1 cl in last sp, sl st to beginning ch-2 (48 sts, or 16 cl).
Round 5: Ch 2, 1 dc, 1 hdc into same sp as ch-2 * 2 cl between next cl, 1 cl in each of next 3 sps between cl *. Repeat from * twice. 2 cl in next sp between cl, 1 cl between each of next 2 cl. Sl st to beginning ch-2 (60 sts or 20 cl).
Rounds 6-22: Ch 2, 1 dc, 1 hdc into same sp as ch-2. 1 cl between each pair of cl in previous row. Sl st to beginning ch-2.

Brim
Change to smaller hook.
Round 1: Ch 1, 2 sc into top of st from previous row. Join ends with sl st to beginning ch.
Rounds 2-4: Ch 1, 1 sc into top of stitch from previous row. Join ends with sl st to beginning ch.

FINISHING
Darn yarn ends into hat and trim.
Using steam and very gentle pressure, block hat and brim into desired shape (see page 137).

These simple beads can be made in many types of yarn to create different textures and use up individual balls from your stash. They are filled with toy stuffing, so are very light to wear. You can play with the pattern by mixing different combinations of yarns and sizes of beads, as well as varying the spacing between them to create a fun and original accessory.

"Marianne" Bead Necklace   Claire Montgomerie

MATERIALS

1 ball Blue Sky Alpacas Alpaca Silk (DK, 50% alpaca, 50% silk, approx. 1¾ oz/50g, 146 yards/133m) in each of the following shades: 139 Peacock, 137 Sapphire, 136 Champagne
Size 2.5mm (B/1½) crochet hook (see page 120)
Toy stuffing, such as polyester fiberfill

MEASUREMENTS

Large beads: Approximately 1¾ inches (4cm) diameter.
Small beads: Approximately 1 inch (2.5cm) diameter.
Length of necklace: Approximately 16 inches (40cm).

GAUGE

Obtaining a certain gauge is not essential, but try to crochet tightly, so that the toy stuffing cannot appear through the holes.

ABBREVIATIONS

See page 120.

NOTE

Use whatever type of yarn and hook you like, to create different beads.

LARGE BEAD

Ch 2, 6 sc in 2nd ch from hook, join round with sl st to first sc.
Round 1: 2 sc in each sc around. 12 sts. Sl st to join.
Round 2: (1 sc in next sc, 2 sc in next sc) around. 18 sts. Sl st to join.
Round 3: Work 1 round straight in sc. Sl st to join.
Round 4: (1 sc into each of next 2 sc, 2 sc in next sc) around. 24 sts. Sl st to join.
Rounds 5-8: Work 4 rows straight in sc. Sl st to join on each row.
Begin stuffing from now, as you start to close sphere, to hold shape.
Round 9: (Decrease by working 2 sc tog, 2 sc) around. 18 sts. Sl st to join.
Round 10: Work 1 row straight in sc. Sl st to join.

Round 11: (Decrease by working 2 sc tog, 1 sc) around. 12 sts. Sl st to join.
Rounds 12 and 13: 2 sc tog around for next row and until you are left with 3 sts.
Fasten off yarn and darn closed.

Make 1 bead of each color for necklace shown, or as many as you wish for a necklace of your own design.

SMALL BEAD

Ch 2, 6 sc in 2nd ch from hook, join round with sl st to first sc.
Round 1: 2 sc in each sc around. 12 sts. Sl st to join.
Round 2: (1 sc in next sc, 2 sc in next sc) around. 18 sts. Sl st to join.
Rounds 3-6: Work 4 rounds straight in sc. Sl st to join at end of each row.
Begin stuffing from now, as you start to close sphere, to hold shape.
Round 7: (Decrease by working 2 sc tog, 1 sc) around. 12 sts. Sl st to join.
Rounds 8-9: 2 sc tog around for next row and until you are left with 3 sts.
Fasten off yarn and darn closed.

Make 3 or 4 beads in each color for necklace shown, or as many as you wish for a necklace of your own design.

CHAIN

Using size 2.5mm (B/1½) hook, chain a length of approximately 32 inches (80cm), or desired length for necklace. Thread all beads onto chain randomly. Join chain with sl st to first ch. Fasten off.

The perfect accessory for all hippie chicks, this wide spike-stitch hairband, with an extra-long tie worked in bobble stitch, looks great with either short or long hair. Wear it with everything from flowing smock dresses to neat mini shifts, from skimpy shorts to slouchy jeans.

"Sienna" Headband   Bee Clinch

MATERIALS
1 ball Blue Sky Alpacas Melange (DK, 100% alpaca, approx. 1¾ oz/50g, 109⅜ yards/100m) in of each of the following shades: 800 Cornflower (yarn A), 809 Toasted Almond (yarn B), 802 Pesto (yarn C), 806 Salsa (yarn D)
Size 3.5mm (E/4) crochet hook (see page 120)
Two vintage buttons, approximately ¾-1¼ inches (2-3cm) diameter
Tapestry needle

MEASUREMENTS
Length: main band 23 inches (58cm); ties 22 inches (56cm) each.
Width, including edging: 4¾ inches (12cm).

GAUGE
10 sts to 2½ inches (6cm) using size 3.5mm (E/4) hook or the size to obtain the correct gauge.

ABBREVIATIONS
See page 120.

SPECIAL ABBREVIATIONS
ssc2—single spiked crochet: (See page 129.) (Be sure to insert hook into center of the spikes 2 rows below the row you are working.) Yo, draw through and up to height of row being worked, yo, draw through both loops on hook.
ps—puff stitch: (See page 123.) To make a puff stitch of 4 half double crochet stitches: yo, insert the hook into the stitch, yo again and draw a loop through (3 loops on the hook).
Repeat this step 3 more times, inserting the hook into the same stitch each time (9 loops on hook), yo 2, and draw through all loops on hook.

NOTE
The sequencing of colors is purely optional, but three different colors must be used for the main piece.

HEADBAND
Measure head from base of right ear to base of left ear. For a band to fit size 18 inches (45cm), using yarn A, ch 72. Adjust size according to yarn gauge; however, note that the spiked stitch pattern must be worked over a multiple 10 + 2 sts.
Row 1 (RS): 1 sc into 2nd ch from hook, sc to end, ch 1, turn.
Row 2: Using yarn B, 1 sc into first st, sc to end, ch 1, turn.
Row 3: 1 sc into first st * 1 ssc2 over each of next 5 sts, 1 sc in next 5 sts; repeat from * ending 1 sc into last sc, ch 1, turn.
Rows 4-9: Repeat the last 2 rows with yarn C, followed with 2 rows in yarn A, then 2 rows in yarn B.
Row 10: Using yarn C, as row 1.
Row 11: 1 sc in first st, * 1 sc in next 5 sts, 1 ssc2 in next 5 sts; repeat from * ending 1 sc in last st, ch 1, turn.
Rows 12-17: Repeat the last 2 rows with yarn A, yarn B, then Yarn C. Repeat entire 17 rows once more. Fasten off.

FINISHING
To miter the ends of the headband, fold the corners at each end toward center of headband to create a triangle at each end. Using yarn and a tapestry needle, sew the mitered ends in place securely.
To picot the edge: Using yarn D and beginning at straight edge, sc into first sc sp on headband, * ch 3, sl st into ch-1 (picot made), sc into next sc on headband; repeat from * along straight edge to start of mitering. Continue with picots around mitered edge with at least 4 picots to each side of miter. Repeat along other edge and miter. Fasten off.
Puff-stitch ties: Using yarn D ch 4.
Row 1: 1 sc into 2nd ch, sc to end, ch 1, turn.
Row 2: 1 sc in first st, ps in next st, 1 sc, ch 1, turn.
Repeat these 2 rows until tie measures approximately 18 inches (45cm), finishing with row 1. Fasten off.
Make another tie to match the first.
Press headband and ties lightly (see page 137).
Sew ties to wrong side of mitered corners of headband.
Sew the buttons on right side of mitered corners.

Nostalgic Home

Wrap this colorful blanket around you for instant comfort and warmth, or throw it over your bed for a homespun country look. The cheerful chevron stripes will lift your spirits and conjure up images of romantic snow-covered cabins in the woods, or cuddling up with a mug of hot chocolate after ice-skating.

Chevron Blanket   Bee Clinch

MATERIALS

6 balls Rowan Cashsoft (DK, 57% extra-fine merino, 33% microfiber, 10% cashmere, approx. 1¾ oz/50g, 142¼ yards/130m) in each of the following shades: 509 Lime (yarn A), 501 Sweet (yarn B), 517 Donkey (yarn C), 502 Bella Donna (yarn D)

Size 4mm (G/6) crochet hook (see page 120)

Tapestry needle

MEASUREMENTS

Approx. 48 x 72 inches (120 x 180cm). Size can be adjusted as required, using a multiple of 12 sts + 3. To make a full-size blanket, you will need twice as much yarn and should cast on twice the number of stitches.

GAUGE

18 sts x 8 rows = 4 inches (10cm) over chevron pattern using size 4mm (G/6) hook or the size required to obtain the correct gauge.

ABBREVIATIONS

See page 120.

SPECIAL ABBREVIATIONS

dc2tog—ridged chevron in double crochet: To work 2 double crochet together, wrap yarn over hook and insert in the next stitch, draw through the loop (3 loops on hook), wrap yarn over hook, draw through first 2 loops on hook (2 loops left on hook). Repeat the step on next stitch (3 loops left on hook). Wrap yarn over hook and draw through all 3 loops to complete group. Working under one loop, insert the hook into the back loop, leaving the other loop as a bar to form a ridge across the row.

BLANKET

Using yarn A ch 216 + 3. Turn.

Row 1: 1 dc in 4th ch from hook, * 1 dc in next 3 ch (over next 2 sts work dc2tog) twice, 1 dc into each of next 3 sts, (2 dc into next st) twice; repeat from * ending last repeat with 2 dc into last ch, turn.

Row 2: Ch 3 (counts as 1 dc), 1 dc into first st, always inserting hook into back loop only of each stitch, * 1 dc into each of next 3 sts, (over next 2 sts work dc2tog) twice, 1 dc into each of next 3 sts, (2 dc into next st) twice; repeat from * ending last repeat with 2 dc once only into top of turning ch, turn. Using yarn B, repeat row 2 twice.

Repeat row 2 twice in yarn C and then in yarn D. This sets the sequence to be repeated in all four colors until throw measures finished length.

FINISHING

Using tapestry needle darn all loose yarn ends into blanket.

Press lightly following yarn label instructions (see page 137).

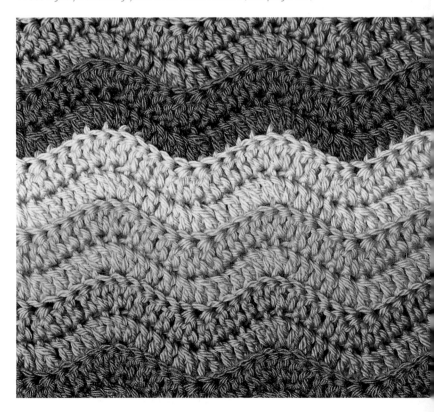

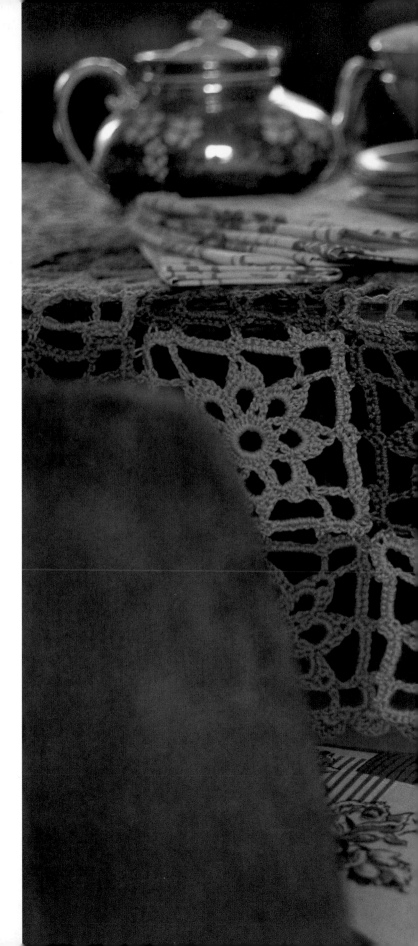

This glorious vintage tablecloth evokes the more relaxed pace of days gone by, when ladies of leisure gathered for afternoon tea, complete with dainty china tea set and home-baked cakes. Perfect for special occasions, or to leave out all the time, this pretty tablecloth, made up of colorful picot squares, adds character to any table. You could also make a narrower version to use as a table runner.

Picot Star Tablecloth

Emma Seddon

MATERIALS

Jaeger Siena 4-Ply Cotton (sportweight, 100% mercerised cotton, approx. 1¾ oz/50g, 153⅛ yards/140m), in the following shades and quantities:
  3 balls shade 412 Sapling (yarn A)
  3 balls shade 432 Clover (yarn B)
  3 balls shade 431 Sage (yarn C)
  3 balls shade 433 Teak (yarn D)
  3 balls shade 417 Blush (yarn E)
  4 balls shade 430 Ocean (yarn F)
Size 3mm (C/2½) crochet hook (see page 120)
Tapestry needle

MEASUREMENTS

Approximately 39 x 49 inches (98 x 124cm).

GAUGE

One square = 5 x 5 inches (12 x 12cm), using size 3mm (C/2½) hook, or the size required to obtain the correct gauge.

ABBREVIATIONS

See page 120.

SPECIAL ABBREVIATIONS

MP—make picot: Ch 3, sl st into same sp.

PICOT SQUARE PATTERN

Make 14 in A.
Make 14 in B.
Make 13 in C.
Make 12 in D.
Make 13 in E.
Make 14 in F.
Total of 80 squares.

Ch 8, sl st to join into ring, ch 1 (see open ring method on page 126).
Round 1: 32 sc into ring, join with sl st.
Round 2: Ch 8 (1 dc in next sc, skip 2 sc, 1 dc in next sc, ch 5) 7 times, 1 dc in next sc, join with sl st to 3rd of 8 ch.
Round 3: Sl st into ch-5 sp, (1 sc, 1 hdc, 2 dc, ch 3, 2 dc, 1 hdc, 2 sc into same ch-5 sp), * (1 sc, 1 hdc, 2 dc, ch 3, 2 dc, 1 hdc, 2 sc into next ch-5 sp), repeat from * 7 more times, join with a sl st to first sc.
Round 4: Sl st along chains, up to next ch-3 loop, 1 sc in same sp, * ch 6, (1 tr, ch 5, 1 tr) in next ch-3 loop, ch 6, 1 sc in next ch-3 loop, repeat from * 3 more times, ch 6, finish last repeat with a sl st into first sc.
Round 5: 1 sc into first sc made, * MP, 6 sc into ch-6 sp, sc into tr, MP, (4 sc, MP, 3 sc into ch-5 sp), 1 sc into tr, MP, 6 sc into ch-6 sp, 1 sc into next sc, repeat from * 3 more times, end last repeat with sl st into first sc.

FINISHING

Block the squares (see page 137).
With WS facing, lay squares out according to following chart. Using a tapestry needle and yarn of your choice, sew the squares together by overcasting picots and corners together, carrying yarn through back of crochet between picots.

B	C	D	E	F	A	B	C
A	B	C	D	E	F	A	B
F	A	B	C	D	E	F	A
E	F	A	B	C	D	E	F
D	E	F	A	B	C	D	E
C	D	E	F	A	B	C	D
B	C	D	E	F	A	B	C
A	B	C	D	E	F	A	B
F	A	B	C	D	E	F	A
E	F	A	B	C	D	E	F

Edging

With RS facing and using yarn F, join yarn to any central picot on a square—not on a corner, as it would be difficult to get a neat corner join.
Ch 3, 4 dc in same sp, skip 2 sc, sl st into next 2 sc, skip 2 sc, 5 dc into picot sp, skip 2 sc, sl st into next 2 sc, 5 dc into join between squares, skip 2 sc, * sl st into next 2 sc, (5 dc into picot sp, skip 2 sc, sl st into next 3 sc) twice, 5 dc into picot sp, skip 2 sc. Repeat from * across each square and along each edge.

Corners: Work 5 dc into corner picot sp as per pattern.

Finish by slip-stitching into the ch-3 first made and joining back to the main fabric of the cloth.

This funky cushion lends a laid-back modern-retro vibe to any living room. The chocolate brown yarn will add a touch of warmth and texture to neutral interiors, and you can add as many of the colorful popcorn stitches as you like.

Popcorn-Stitch Cushion   Nicki Trench with Zara Poole

MATERIALS
Debbie Bliss Cashmerino Chunky (55% merino wool, 33% microfiber, 12% cashmere, approx. 1¾ oz/50g, 71 yards/65m) in the following shades and quantities: 6 balls shade 15 Chocolate Brown (yarn A), 2 balls shade 11 Pale Blue (yarn B), 2 balls shade 12 Pale Green (yarn C)
Size 7mm (K/10½)crochet hook (see page 120)
Tapestry needle
Mother-of-pearl button, approximately 1¼ inches (3cm) diameter
Round pillow form, 17 inches (43cm) in diameter
Small pompom maker or cardboard to make template (see page 136)

GAUGE
12 dc = 4 inches (10cm) using size 7mm (K/10½) hook.

SPECIAL ABBREVIATIONS (See page 120 for standard abbreviations)
pc–popcorn: Work 4 dc in the same place, slip the last loop off the hook. Reinsert the hook in the top of the first dc of the group and catch the empty loop. Pull this loop through to close the popcorn.

CUSHION COVER
Make 2 sides. Work popcorns on front of cushion in yarns B and C; alternate colors for each popcorn, picking up new color on last pull-through of previous stitch. Work popcorns on back of cushion in yarn A.
Using yarn A ch 6 and join with sl st to form a ring.
Round 1: Ch 3, 11 dc into ring, join with sl st to top of ch-3.
Round 2: Ch 3, 1 dc in same st, * 2 dc into next st, repeat from * to end, join with sl st to top of ch-3. 24 sts.
Round 3: Ch 3, 1 dc in same st, * 1 dc in next st, 2 dc in next st twice, repeat from * to end, join with sl st to top of ch-3. 40 sts.
Round 4: Ch 3, 1 dc in same st, * 1 dc in next 3 sts, 2 dc in next st, repeat from * to last 3 sts, 1 dc in last 3 sts, join with sl st to top of ch-3. 50 sts.
Round 5: Ch 3, 1 dc in same st, change to yarn C and work * 1 pc in next st, change to yarn A, 1 dc in next 4 sts, repeat from * to last 3 sts, 1 dc in next 3 sts, join with sl st to top of ch-3.
Round 6: Ch 3, 1 dc in same st, * 1 dc in next 5 sts, 2 dc in next st, repeat from * to last 6 sts, 1 dc in next 6 sts, join with sl st to top of ch-3.
Round 7: Ch 3, 1 dc in same st, change to yarn B and work * 1 pc in next st, change to yarn A and work 1 dc in next 6 sts, repeat from * to end, join with sl st to top of ch-3.
Round 8: Ch 3, 1 dc in same st, * 1 dc in next 7 sts, 2 dc in next st, repeat from * to last 9 sts, 1 dc in next 9 sts, join with sl st to top of ch-3.
Round 9: Ch 3, 1 dc in same st, * 1 dc in next 8 sts, change to yarn C, 1 pc in next st, change to yarn A, repeat from * to end, join with sl st to top of ch-3.
Round 10: Ch 3, 1 dc in same st, * 1 dc in next 9 sts, 2 dc in next st, repeat from * to last 12 sts, 1 dc in next 12 sts, join with sl st to top of ch-3.
Round 11: Ch 3, 1 dc in same st, 1 dc in next 6 sts, change to yarn B, 1 pc in next st, change to Yarn A, 1 dc in next 10 sts, repeat from * to last 6 sts, 1 dc in next 6 sts, join with sl st to top of ch-3.
Round 12: Ch 3, 1 dc in same st, * 1 dc in next 4 sts, 2 dc in next st, repeat from * to last 2 sts, 1 dc in next 2 sts, join with sl st to top of ch-3. Fasten off.

Central flower
Using yarn C ch 6.
Round 1: Ch 3 (counts as first dc), * ch 2, 1 dc into ring, rep from * 6 times, ch 2, join with sl st to top of ch-3.
Round 2: Into each ch-2 sp work (1 sc, 1 hdc, 3 dc, 1 hdc, 1 sc), join with sl st to sl st at end of round 1.
Round 3: * Ch 4, keeping chain behind petals of round 2, 1 sc into back of next dc on round 1, repeat from * 6 times, join with sl st to sl st at end of round 2.
Round 4: Into each ch-4 loop work (1 sc, 1 hdc, 5 dc, 1 hdc, 1 sc), join with sl st to sl st at end of round 3.
Round 5: As round 3, working into the back of sc on round 3. Fasten off.
Round 6: Join yarn C to sl st at end of last round. Into each ch-4 loop work (1 sc, 1 hdc 7 dc, 1 hdc, 1 sc), join with sl st to sl st at end of round 5.
Round 7: As round 3, working into sc of round 5.
Round 8: Into each ch-4 loop work (1 sc, 1 hdc, 2 dc, 5 tr, 2dc , 1 hdc, 1 sc), join with sl st to sl st at end of round 7. Fasten off.
Darn in ends and sew flower on cushion. Sew button in center of flower.

FINISHING
Place wrong sides together and join with 1 row sc. Work two-thirds of the way around, insert pillow form, and continue rest of sc row. Fasten off.
Make 10 pompoms, approx. 5 inches (12cm) diameter, in a mixture of yarns B and C, and sew to seam at regular intervals (see page 136).

THE OBSERVER'S BOOK
OF
WILD FLOWERS

This pretty shelf runner is the kind that would have graced the pantries and kitchen dressers of our grandmothers and great-grandmothers. It is ideal for dressing up open shelves in modern kitchens and makes the perfect backdrop for an array of vintage china and kitchenware. Have fun embellishing it with a variety of buttons, charms, or beads.

Shelf Runner

Emma Seddon

MATERIALS

1 ball Blue Sky Alpacas Sportweight (100% baby alpaca, approx. 1¾ oz/50g 109⅜ yards/100m) in each of the following shades: 500 Natural White (yarn A), 47 Green (yarn B)
Size 3.5mm (E/4) crochet hook (see page 120)
Fabric the size of the shelf, plus ¾ inch (2cm) hem allowance around each edge
Buttons for decoration
Tapestry needle
Chenille needle (optional)

MEASUREMENTS

Width of crochet edging: 2¾ inches (7cm).

GAUGE

Obtaining a certain gauge is not essential.

ABBREVIATIONS

See page 120.

SHELF RUNNER

Press under ¾ inch (2cm) along all edges of the fabric.
Using a tapestry or chenille needle and yarn A, work blanket stitch along the edge of the fabric, keeping the stitches small and close together (see page 134).

CROCHETED EDGES

Row 1: With RS toward you, join in yarn A by working single crochet into each blanket-stitch loop. You need to end up with a multiple of 4 stitches, plus 1 to make repeat, so you may need to sc into same space twice to get the correct number of sts. Fasten off.
Row 2: With RS toward you, join in yarn B. Ch 4, * skip 1 ch, 1 dc into next ch, ch 1. Repeat from * to end. Fasten off.
Row 3: With WS toward you, join in yarn A to first ch-1 sp, ch 5, dc into same space, * skip next ch-1 sp, (1 dc, ch 2, 1 dc) into next ch-1 sp, rep from *. Turn.
Row 4: Sl st into ch-2 sp, (2 sc, ch 3, 2 sc) into same sp, * sl st into space between dc, (2 sc, ch 3, 2 sc) into next ch-2 sp. Repeat from *. Fasten off.
Row 5: With WS toward you, join in yarn B to ch-3 sp at end of point. Ch 5, dc into same sp, * (1 dc, ch 2, 1 dc) into next ch-3 sp, rep from *. Turn.
Row 6: As row 4.
Row 7: With RS facing, join in yarn A to first sc, sl st into next ch, * (1 sc, 1 hdc, 1 dc, 2 ch, 1 dc, 1 hdc, 1 sc) into ch-3 sp, sl st into next 2 ch, sl st into space between dc, ch 3, sl st back into space between dc, sl st into next 2 chain. Repeat from *. Fasten off.

FINISHING

Darn in ends using a tapestry needle.
Lay out shelf runner and place buttons (or beads, if you prefer) evenly over the crocheted edge of the runner.
To attach the buttons, first thread a separate length of yarn A through each button; check that the button will face outward when hanging by evening up the two ends of the yarn and holding each button up. Tie a knot at the top of the button to secure the yarn, and use the tapestry needle to sew the ends into the underside of the adjacent crochet stitches.

Decorated with clusters of exquisite Turkish "Oya" needle-lace flowers attached at intervals along the bottom edge, this café curtain brings a quirky retro touch to a small window. It is attached at half height, making it ideal for use in a kitchen or bathroom, where it will offer some degree of privacy but still let in natural light. As an alternative trim, use crochet flowers, pompoms, fringe, or buttons.

Café Curtain

Nicki Trench with Zara Poole

MATERIALS

ggh Safari (worsted, 78% linen, 22% polyamide, approx. 1¾ oz/50g, 153⅛ yards/140m) in the following shades and quantities:
4 balls shade 36 Green (yarn A), 1 ball shade 41 Rust (yarn B)
Size 3mm (C/2½) crochet hook (see page 120)
Turkish "Oya" needle-lace flowers (or other embellishments)
Needle and sewing thread

MEASUREMENTS

24 inches (60cm) wide, 18 inches (45cm) deep.

GAUGE

3 complete shell repeats = 4 inches (10cm) using size 3mm (C/21/2) hook or the size required to obtain the correct gauge.

ABBREVIATIONS

See page 120.

CURTAIN PANEL

The pattern is based on a multiple of 7 ch plus 2 ch, plus 2 ch on foundation row.
Using yarn A ch 116.
Row 1: 1 dc in 4th ch from hook, * skip 2 ch, 5 dc in next ch, skip 2 ch, 1 dc in each of next 2 ch, repeat from * to end, turn.
Row 2: Ch 3, 2 dc in first dc, skip 3 dc, * 1 dc in space between 2nd and 3rd dc of group, 1 dc in sp between 3rd and 4th dc of group, skip 3 dc, 5 dc in sp between 2 vertical dc, skip 3 dc, repeat from *, ending 3 dc in sp between last dc and 3 ch, turn.
Row 3: Ch 3, 1 dc between first 2 dc, * skip 3 dc, 5 dc in space between 2 vertical dc, skip 3 dc, 1 dc in sp between 2nd and 3rd dc of group, 1 dc in sp between 3rd and 4th dc of group, repeat from *, ending 1 dc in sp between last dc and 3 ch, 1 dc in 3rd of 3 ch, turn.
Repeat rows 2 and 3 until work measures 18 inches (45cm). Fasten off.

FINISHING

Finish with a row of sc worked all the way around the top and sides in yarn A and along the bottom in yarn B.
Block following the instructions on page 137.
Use yarn B to attach clusters of lace flowers (or other embellishment of your choice) at intervals.

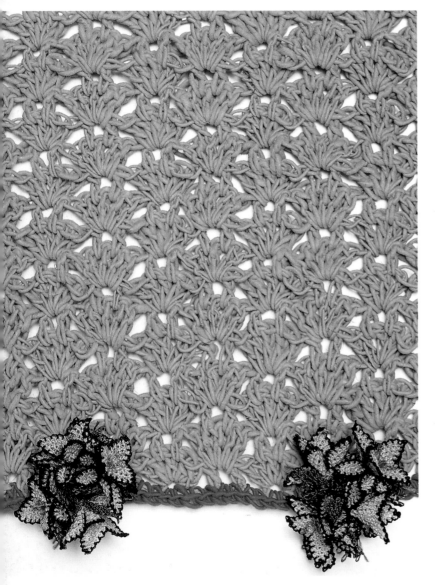

This funky lampshade, in a gorgeous combination of chestnut, ginger, mandarin, and kiwi, will add instant warmth, as well as a retro touch, to a room. It is made in sections, which means you can crochet as many or as few flowers as you need to cover your own style of shade. Sew the cover to the outside of an existing shade to limit the (minimal) risk of overheating.

Twinkle Lampshade

Claire Montgomerie

MATERIALS

Blue Sky Alpacas Silk (DK, 50% alpaca, 50% silk, approx. 1¾ oz/50g, 146 yards/133m) in the following shades and quantities:
   3 balls shade 130 Mandarin (yarn A), 5 balls shade 131 Kiwi (yarn B), 3 balls shade 132 Ginger (yarn C), 3 balls shade 135 Chestnut (yarn D)
Size 4.5mm (G/7) crochet hook (see page 120)
Lampshade: 8 inches (20cm) tall, 12 inches (30cm) diameter
Chenille needle and matching thread

GAUGE

Flowers measure approximately 4 inches (10cm) diameter, worked on size 4.5mm (G/6/7) hook; however the correct gauge is not essential.

ABBREVIATIONS

See page 120.

FLOWERS

For the flowers, tie in the colors as randomly or as regularly as you wish, using a different color for each visible round, keeping each flower one color or a mixture. Here the flower colors are somewhat randomly chosen; but generally use yarn B (Kiwi) for the two lower base rounds, swapping the remaining colors as you please for the top two rounds.

Using the finger method (see page 127), make a ring for the center of each flower. Wrap the yarn around three fingers (or a knitting needle of approximately 20mm [¾ inch]) 20 times.
Round 1: Work 36 sc into ring evenly so all wrapped yarn is covered. Join with sl st to first sc. Fasten off.

Round 2: Fasten in next yarn. * Ch 6, skip 5 sc, 1 sl st into next sc, rep from * 5 times, ending with sl st into bottom of first ch. 6 loops.
Round 3: * Work (1 sc, 2 hdc, 11 dc, 2 hdc, 1 sc) into first loop sp, sl st to sl st, rep from * for next 5 ch loops. Fasten off. 6 petals.
Round 4: Attach next yarn and * ch 6, sl st into sl st of round 2, rep from * 5 times. 6 loops.
Round 5: * Work (1 sc, 2 hdc, 11 dc, 2 hdc, 1 sc) into ch loop, sl st to sl st, rep from * for next 5 ch loops. Fasten off. 6 petals.
Round 6: Attach next yarn and * ch 8, sl st into sl st of round 2, rep from * 5 times. 6 loops.
Round 7: Work (1 sc, 2 hdc, 15 dc, 2 hdc, 1 sc) into ch loop, sl st to sl st, rep from * for next 5 ch loops. Fasten off. 6 petals.
Round 8: Still continuing with yarn used for round 7, attach yarn to a sc of round 1 that is centered between the 2 sl sts of 1 petal from round 2, so that the next petals will be between the petals of previous rounds. * Ch 10, sl st into central sc between petal of round 2, rep from * 5 more times. 6 loops.
Round 9: Work (1 sc, 2 hdc, 19 dc, 2 hdc, 1 sc) into ch loop, sl st to sl st, rep from * for next 5 ch loops. Fasten off yarn (6 petals).

Make enough flowers to cover your chosen lampshade as densely as you would like. The shade shown required 30 flowers.

FINISHING

Sew all flowers together into a strip by the lowest layer of petals, joining by the central (10th) dc. Attach to lampshade either by sewing directly onto it using a chenille needle and matching sewing thread or by working ch 3 at the top and ch 3 at the bottom and then tying them on the inside of the shade..

The subtle pastel colors of Jordan almonds inspired this pretty breakfast set, including cozies to keep coffee, tea, and boiled eggs warm. The ritual of a traditional family breakfast is a lovely way to wake up and start the day, especially on lazy weekends.

Kate's Breakfast Set

Kate Samphier

MATERIALS

For tea cozy

1 ball Blue Sky Alpacas Sportweight (100% baby alpaca, approx. 1¾ oz/50g, 109⅜ yards/100m) in each of the following shades: 514 Pale Aqua (yarn A), 506 Natural Streaky Brown (yarn B)

Size 5mm (H/8) crochet hook (see page 120)

For French press coffeepot cozy

1 ball Blue Sky Alpacas Sportweight (100% baby alpaca, approx. 1¾ oz/50g, 109⅜ yards/100m) in each of the following shades: 515 Pistachio (yarn A), 506 Natural Streaky Brown (yarn B) (for contrast picot trim)

Size 4.5mm (G/7) crochet hook (see page 120)

3 vintage buttons, approximately 1¼ inches (3cm) diameter

Needle and sewing thread

For egg cozies

1 ball Blue Sky Alpacas Sportweight (100% baby alpaca, approx. 1¾ oz/50g, 109⅜ yards/100m) in each of the following shades for 6 cozies (2 in each color): 505 Natural Taupe (yarn A), 514 Pale Aqua (yarn B), 500 Natural White (yarn C); 1 ball shade 506 Natural Streaky Brown (yarn D) (for contrast picot trim)

Size 4.5mm (G/7) crochet hook

One vintage button for each cozy, ½–⅝ inch (10-15mm) diameter

Needle and thread

MEASUREMENTS

Tea cozy: 5½ inches (14cm) deep; 8 inches (20cm) diameter at rim.

Coffeepot cozy: 5 inches (13cm) deep; 12 inches (30cm) long.

Egg cozy: 2½ inches (6cm) deep; 3 inches (8cm) diameter at bottom edge.

GAUGE

For tea cozy: 1 motif = 1¼ inches (3cm), using size 5mm (H/8) crochet hook.

17 st to 4 inches (10cm) using a size 4.5mm (G/7) crochet hook.

Change hook size(s) if necessary to obtain the correct gauge.

ABBREVIATIONS

See page 120.

TEA COZY

Using yarn B and larger hook, ch 32.

Row 1: 1 sc in 2nd ch from hook, 1 sc in each ch to end. 31 sts. Change to yarn A.

Row 2 (WS): Ch 3, * skip 3 sts, 3 dc in next st, (group made); rep from * to last 3 sts, skip 2 sts, 1 dc in last st.

Row 3: Ch 1, 1 sc in first st, 2 dc in next free st of 2 rows below (working around sts of previous row), * 1 sc in center of group of 3 dc, 3 dc in center of 3 free sts, of 2 rows below; rep from * ending 1 sc in center dc of last group, 2 dc in center of 3 free sts, 1 sc in top of ch-3.

Row 4: As row 1.

Row 5: As row 2.

Rows 6-14: Repeat rows 2-5 twice more, then row 1 again.

Row 15: Ch 1, 1 sc in first st, 2 dc in next free st, * 1 sc in center dc of next group, 2 dc in center free st, rep from * to end, 1 sc in top of ch-3. Change to Yarn B

Row 16: Ch 3, * skip 1 st, dec 1; rep from * ending 1 dc in last st.

Row 17: Ch 3, * dec 1; rep from * ending 1 dc in top of ch-3. Fasten off. Make another piece in the same way.

Join seams (see page 137), leaving openings for spout and handle.

COFFEEPOT COZY

Using yarn A and smaller hook, ch 49.

Row 1: Work in sc.

Continue to work rows of sc until work measures 4½ inches (11cm) from starting edge. Fasten off.

Picot edge

Join in yarn B and, working into loops from previous row, * ch 3, 1 sc in first of these ch, skip 1 st, 1 sc in next st; rep from * to end. Fasten off. Join yarn B to bottom edge. Work picot edge to match above. Fasten off.

Button loops

Using yarn B work 3 button loops in ch, to the size appropriate for your chosen buttons. Sew onto edge of cozy.

Using needle and thread, sew buttons along opposite edge to correspond to button loops.

EGG COZY (Make 2 cozies in each of yarns A, B, and C)

Using yarn A and smaller hook, ch 3, join into ring with sl st.

Round 1: 6 sc into ring.

Round 2: (2 sc in each st) 6 times. 12 sts.

Round 3: (1 sc in next st, 2 sc in next st) 6 times. 18 sts.

Round 4: (1 sc in each of next 2 sts, 2 sc in next st) 6 times. 24 sts.

Rounds 5-7: Work 5 rounds sc.

Round 8: Change to contrasting yarn D, * ch 3, 1 sc in first of these ch, skip 1 st, 1 sc in next st; rep from * to end. Fasten off.

Repeat to make another cozy in yarn A, then make 4 more cozies using yarns B and C.

Using a needle and thread, sew a vintage button to the top of each egg cozy.

Lazy Summers

Vintage-style patterned cotton fabric, ripped into strips and used instead of conventional yarn, gives this picnic blanket tons of character, as well as making it strong and functional. The edging has been worked in a natural linen yarn, which adds to the rustic appeal. On the next sunny day, roll up the blanket, pack up your hamper and head for the nearest meadow, beach, or park—or take it on a camping trip.

Picnic Blanket

Bee Clinch

MATERIALS
3 "cheese" (reels) Texere Natural Pure Linen Fancy (100% pure natural linen, approx. 14 oz/400g, 1094 yards/1000m), shade Silver & White
10 yards (9m) cotton fabric, torn into twenty $\frac{1}{16}$-inch (2mm) strips and the rest into $\frac{1}{8}$-inch (3mm) strips
Sizes 5.5mm (I/9) and 15mm (Q) crochet hooks
Tapestry needle

MEASUREMENTS
Inner square: $24\frac{1}{2}$ x $24\frac{1}{2}$ inches (62 x 62cm).
Finished blanket: 52 x 52 inches (132 x 132cm).

GAUGE
Each square = 13 x 13 inches (33 x 33cm) using linen yarn and a size 5.5mm (I/9) hook.
4 sts = 4 inches (10cm) using $\frac{1}{8}$ inch (3mm) fabric strips and a size 15mm (Q) hook Change hook size if necessary to obtain the correct gauge.

ABBREVIATIONS
See page 120.

SPECIAL ABBREVIATIONS
frdc—front raised double crochet; also known as "cable stitch":
Yarn over hook and insert from front to back around post of next sc 2nd round down, draw up a $\frac{1}{2}$-inch (1cm) loop, yo and pull through 2 loops twice.

NOTES
Depending on your preference, the size of the blanket can be increased by adding more squares and adapting the size of the central fabric square. More yarn and fabric will have to be purchased according to the size you wish to make.

To make fabric strips: Tear down the length of the fabric at $\frac{1}{8}$-inch (3mm) intervals to create fabric "yarn" (make a small cut with scissors to start the tear). In the same way, tear 20 strips $\frac{1}{16}$ inch (2mm) wide for the contrasting rounds in the square motif.

LINEN SQUARE MOTIF (Make 12)
Using linen yarn and smaller hook, ch 4, join with sl st into ring.
Round 1: Ch 1, 8 sc into ring, join in with sl st to first sc. Turn. Turn at end of every round.
Round 2: Ch 1, 1 sc in joined stitch, 1 sc in next sc, * (corner group of 1 sc, ch 2, 1 sc) in next sc, 1 sc in next sc, repeat from * around; sl st in first sc (3 sts per side).
Round 3: Ch 1, 1 sc in joining sc, 1 sc in each st to ch-2 sp at corner, * a corner group in ch-2 sp, 1 sc in each st to next ch-2 sp, repeat from * around; sl st in first sc (5 sts per side).
Rounds 4–9: Repeat round 3 six times (17 sts per side).
Fasten off.
Round 10: Using $\frac{1}{16}$-inch (2mm) fabric strip and smaller hook, ch 1, work 1 sc in joining sc; continue as in round 3 but change back to linen yarn in last sc (19 sts per side).

Round 11 (RS): Continuing in linen yarn, ch 1, 1 sc in joining sc, * 1 sc in each of next 5 sc, frdc in next sc, 1 sc in each of next 7 sc, work a frdc st, 1 sc in each of next 5 sc, a corner group in next ch-2 sp, repeat from * around omitting corner group from last repeat; sl st in 1st sc (21 sts per side).

Round 12: Repeat round 3 (23 sts per side).

Round 13: Ch 1, 1 sc in joining sc, * 1 sc in each of next 7 sc, frdc around cable stitch below, 1 sc in each of next 7 sc, frdc around cable stitch below, 1 sc in each of next 7 sc, a corner group in ch-2 sp: repeat from * around, ending and joining as before (25 sts per side).

Round 14: Repeat round 3 (27 sts per side).

Round 15: Ch 1, 1 sc in joining sc, * 1 sc in each of next 9 sc, frdc as before, 1 sc in each of next 7 sc, frdc as before, 1 sc in each of next 9 sc, a corner group in ch-2 sp: repeat from * around, ending and joining as before. Fasten off.

Make 11 more squares.

CENTRAL FABRIC SQUARE

Using ⅛-inch (3mm) fabric strip and larger hook, ch 30 + 1. Turn.

Row 1: Sc in 2nd st from hook, continue in sc to end. Ch 1, turn.

Repeat row 1 until work measures 26 inches (66cm).

FINISHING

Join the linen square motifs together with sc, forming a frame shape with 4 squares along each side.

Join frame to central fabric square with sc.

Sew in loose ends. Press.

Now pack your hamper and fill your flask!

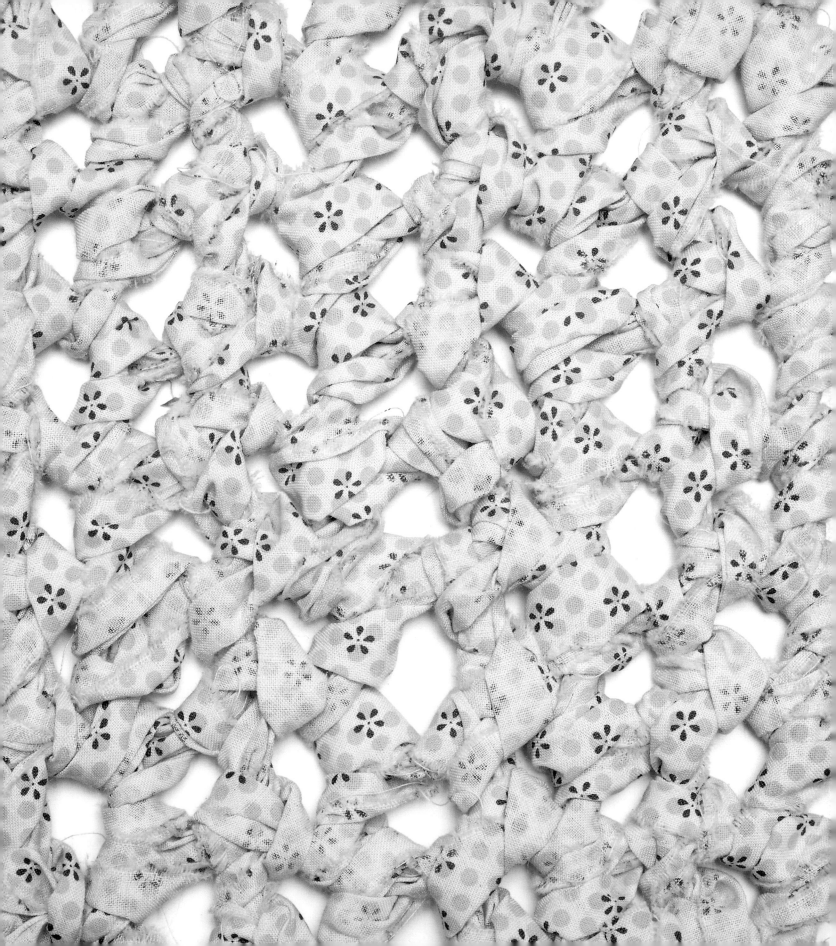

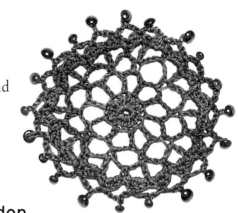

Keep bugs and falling leaves out of your food and drink when eating alfresco by using this great selection of covers for jars, bowls, glasses, and pitchers. This project provides a great opportunity to make samples and try out new stitches on a small scale. Embellish as you like with vintage buttons or charms to weight the covers down.

Assortment of Covers   Emma Seddon

MATERIALS

1 ball Be Sweet Bamboo (100% bamboo, approx. 1¾ oz/50g, 120 yards/110m) in each of the following shades: 645 Pale Lilac (yarn A), 644 Dark Lilac (yarn B), 613 Deep Orange (yarn C), 627 Celery (yarn D), 655 Shell Pink (yarn E)

Size 4mm (G/6) crochet hook

Selection of small buttons, ½–¾ inch (1–2cm) diameter (see individual patterns for number required)

Tapestry needle

MEASUREMENTS

Sugar bowl cover: 5½ inches (14cm) diameter.

Fruit bowl cover: 10 inches (25cm) diameter.

Tumbler cover: 6½ inches (16cm) diameter.

Milk pitcher cover: 9 inches (23cm) diameter.

Salad bowl cover: 13 inches (33cm) diameter.

GAUGE

Obtaining a certain gauge is not essential.

ABBREVIATIONS

See page 120.

SUGAR BOWL COVER (Above right)

Using yarn A thread on 20 assorted buttons.

Ch 4, join with sl st into circle.

Round 1: Ch 3, 10 dc into circle, join with sl st into circle.

Round 2: Ch 6, 1 dc into next chain after sl st, * ch 3, 1 dc into next chain, repeat from *, ch 3, sl st into 3rd ch of ch-6 at beginning of round.

Round 3: Sl st into next ch-3 sp, 1 sc into same sp, * ch 5, 1 sc in next ch-3 sp, rep from *, ch 5, sl st into first sc.

Round 4: Ch 2, sl st into next ch-5 sp, 1 sc into same sp, * ch 3, 1 dc into top of sc (on row below), ch 3, 1 sc into center of ch-5 sp, rep

from *, ch 3, 1 dc into sc (on row below), ch 3, sl st into first sc.

Round 5: (1 hdc, 1 dc, 1 hdc) into same ch-3 sp as sl st, * sl st into dc on previous row, (1 hdc, 1 dc, 1 hdc) into next ch-3 sp, sl st into sc on previous round, repeat from *, sl st into first sc.

Round 6: Sl st along next 2 sts, (you'll be above the dc), * ch 3, push button into position, ch 2, sl st into dc at center of next scallop, repeat from *, ch 3, push button into place, ch 2, sl st into sp at start of round. Fasten off and darn in ends.

FRUIT BOWL COVER (Opposite center)

Using Yarn B thread on 17 assorted buttons

Ch 4, join with sl st into a circle.

Round 1: Ch 5 (counts as 1 dc, ch 2), * 1 dc, ch 2, repeat from * 6 times, join with sl st to 3rd ch of ch-5 at beginning of round.

Round 2: Sl st into first ch-2 sp, ch 3, 2 dc in same sp, * 3 dc into each ch-2 sp, repeat from *, sl st to top of first dc.

Round 3: Ch 6, (1 dc in each of next 3 ch, working only first 2 loops on each st and holding remaining loops on hook, yo and pull through all 4 loops on hook = 1 cluster made), * ch 3, 1 dc between clusters, ch 3, work 1 cluster, repeat from *, ch 3, sl st into 3rd ch of ch-6 ch at beginning of round.

Round 4: Sl st into first sp, sc into same sp, * ch 6, 1 sc into next ch-3 sp, repeat from *, ch 6, sl st to first sc.

Round 5: Sl st along first 3 ch of ch-6, 1 sc into same ch-6 sp, * ch 6, 1 sc into next ch-6 sp, repeat from *, ch 6, sl st into first sc.

Round 6: Sl st along first 3 ch of ch-6, 1 sc into same ch-6 sp, * ch 7, 1 sc into next ch-6 sp, repeat from *, ch 7, sl st into first sc.

Round 7: Sl st along first 3 ch of ch-7, 1 sc into same ch-7 sp, * ch 7, 1 sc into next ch-7 sp, ch 7, sl st to first sc.

Round 8: Sl st along first 3 ch of ch 7, 1 sc into same ch-7 sp, * ch 8, 1 sc in next ch-7 sp, * ch 8, sl st into first sc.

Round 9: Sl st along first 4 ch of ch-8, 1 sc into same ch-8 sp, * ch 8, 1 sc into next ch-8 sp, repeat from * ch 8, sl st into first sc.

Round 10: Turn. With WS toward you, ch 2, push button into place, ch 3, sl st back to sl st at end of last round, * (ch 3, skip 2 ch, sl st into next ch, 3 ch, skip 2 ch, 3 ch, skip 2 ch) along 8 ch, sl st into sc in between 8-ch sps, ch 2, push button into position, ch 3, sl st back into same sc, repeat from * to end, (ch 3, skip 2 ch, sl st into next ch, ch 3, skip 2 ch, ch 3, skip 2 ch) along 8 ch, sl st into first sc. Fasten off and darn in ends.

TUMBLER COVER (Below)

Using yarn C thread on 22 assorted buttons.
Ch 5, join with sl st into a circle.

Round 1: Ch 1, 14 sc into circle, join with sl st to first sc.

Round 2: Ch 2, 1 dc in same sp pulling through first 2 loops, (leaving 2 loops on hook), (work 2 dc, by pulling through first 2 loops on each st, leaving last loop on hook) into next ch, (4 loops on hook), yo and pull through all 4 loops, * ch 3, (2 dc, pull through first 2 loops on each st, leaving last loop on hook) into next 2 ch, (5 loops on hook), yo and pull through all 5 loops, (1 cluster made), repeat from * 6 times, ch 3, sl st to top of first cluster.

Round 3: Sl st into next ch-3 sp, 4 sc into same ch-3 sp, * 4 sc into next ch-3 sp, repeat from *, join with sl st into first sc.

Round 4: Ch 5, * 1 tr in next sc, ch 1, repeat from *, sl st into 4th ch of ch-5 at beginning of round.

Round 5: Ch 2, 1 dc in same sp as sl st, * ch 3, skip next 1 ch, work sl st, ch 3, skip 2 sts (work 3 dc, working first 2 loops of each st, and leaving last loops on hook, yo and pull through all 4 loops on hook = 1 cluster worked), repeat from * ch 3, skip 1 ch, sl st in next ch, ch 3, sl st in top of first dc.

Round 6: * Ch 4, work 1 cluster in same place as sl st worked between clusters on previous round, ch 4, sl st in top of next cluster on previous round, repeat from * ch 4, work 1 cluster in same place as sl st worked between clusters on previous round, ch 4, sl st into same place as first sl st on round.

Round 7: Turn work with WS facing and work ch 1, * (1 sc in next ch-4 sp, ch 2, push button into place, ch 3, 1 sc in same ch-4 sp, ch 1), repeat from *, sl st to first sc in round. Fasten off and darn in ends.

MILK PITCHER COVER (Opposite top)

Using yarn D thread on 29 mother-of-pearl buttons.
Ch 4, join with sl st into circle, ch 1.

Round 1: 10 sc into circle, join with sl st into a circle.

Round 2: Ch 4, * 1 dc into next sc, ch 1, repeat from *, sl st into 3rd ch of ch-4 at beginning of round.

Round 3: Ch 5, * skip 1 ch, 1 dc into top of next dc of round below, ch 2, repeat from *, sl st into 3rd ch of ch-5 at beginning of round.

Round 4: Sl st into first ch-2 sp, 4 sc into each ch-2 sp, sl st into first sc.

Round 5: Ch 4, * 1 dc into next sc, ch 1, rep from *, join with sl st to 3rd ch of ch-4 at beginning of round.

Round 6: Ch 3, dc into same sp as sl st, ch 2, * skip 2 sts, (make 1 dc, leaving 2 loops on hook, make another dc into same sp, pull hook through all 3 loops at once = 1 cluster), ch 2, repeat from *, join with sl st to top of first cluster.

Round 7: Sl st into next ch-2 sp, ch 2, 1 dc in same ch-2 sp, * ch 3, make 1 cluster in next ch-2 sp, repeat from *, ch 3, sl st into top of first cluster.

Round 8: Sl st into next ch-3 sp, ch 2, 2 dc into same ch-3 sp, (working only the first 2 loops of each dc, leaving other loops on hook, yo, pull hook through all 3 loops), * ch 3, (3 dc, pulling loop through first 2 loops of each st, holding remaining loops on hook, yo, hook through all 4 loops = 1 cluster) in each ch-3 sp, repeat from *, ch 3, sl st into top of first cluster.

Round 9: * Ch 6, push button into place, ch 1, sl st back along 2 ch before button, ch 4, sl st into top of next cluster, repeat from *, finish last repeat with sl st into same place as round started. Fasten off and darn in ends.

SALAD BOWL COVER (Below)

Using yarn E thread on 43 buttons.

Ch 4, join with sl st into circle, ch 1.

10 sc into circle, join with sl st into a circle.

Round 1: Ch 3, 1 dc into sp where sl st just made, * ch 2, (work 1 dc, leaving last 2 loops on hook, work next dc and pull through all 3 loops at once in next ch = 1 cluster worked), repeat from *, ch 2, join with sl st to top of ch-3 at beginning of round.

Round 2: Sl st along tops of chains to ch-2 sp, * 3 sc into ch-2 sp, repeat from * to end of round, sl st into top of first sc made.

Round 3: Sl st into next st, ch 3, 4 dc into same sp as sl st, * skip 2 sts, work 5 dc into next ch (center sc of 3 sc), repeat from *, sl st into top of first ch-3.

Round 4: Ch 4, * (1 dc into next st, ch 1) 3 times, 1 dc into next st, skip 1 st, repeat from * to end, sl st into 3rd ch of ch-4 at beginning of round.

Round 5: Ch 1 ch, sc into next ch-1 sp, * ch 3, sc into next ch-1 sp, sc into next ch-1 sp, repeat from *, ch 3, sl st into first sc.

Round 6: Sl st into next ch-3 loop, sc into same sp, * ch 4, sc into next ch-3 loop, repeat from *, ch 4, sl st into first sc.

Round 7: Sl st into next ch-4 sp, (2 sc, ch 3, 2 sc) into same ch-4 sp as sl st, * (2 sc, ch 3, 2 sc) into next ch-4 sp, repeat from * sl st into first sc.

Round 8: Sl st along top of next 2 sts to ch-3 sp, ch 3, 4 dc into same ch-3 sp as sl st, * 5 dc in next ch-3 sp, repeat from * sl st into top of first ch-3.

Round 9: Ch 4, * (1 dc into next ch, ch 1) 3 times, 1 dc in next ch, skip 1 ch, repeat from *, sl st in top of 3rd ch of ch-4 at beginning of round.

Round 10: Repeat round 5.

Round 11: Repeat round 6.

Round 12: Sl st into next ch-4 sp, (2 sc, ch 1, 2 sc) into same 4-ch sp as sl st, * (2 sc, ch 1, 2 sc) into next ch-4 sp, repeat from *, sl st into first sc.

Round 13: Sl st along top of next 2 sts to ch-1 sp, ch 3, 3 dc into same ch-1 sp as sl st, * 4 dc in next ch-1 sp, repeat from *, sl st into top of ch-3 at beginning of round.

Round 14: * Ch 4, push button into place, ch 5, 1 sc into sp between 4 dc of previous row, repeat from *. Fasten off and darn in ends.

This pretty shell-stitch tablecloth is perfect for alfresco breakfast or lunch. Crocheted balls filled with small weights are attached at each corner and along the edges of the cloth, to help prevent it from flying away in the breeze. The crocheted balls are echoed by the jaunty polka-dot design, worked in alternating blue and green.

Garden Tablecloth

Nicki Trench with Zara Poole

MATERIALS
Debbie Bliss Cotton DK (100% cotton, approx. 1¾ oz/50g, 95 yards/
    84m) in the following shades and quantities: 23 balls shade 02 Cream
    (yarn A), 2 balls shade 20 Green (yarn B), 2 balls shade 09 Blue
    (yarn C)
Size 7mm (K/10¾) crochet hook (see page 120)
12 small weights, such as ball bearings

MEASUREMENTS
44 x 36 inches (112 x 92cm).

GAUGE
Yarn gauge 20 stitches to 4 inches (10cm) and 28 rows. Obtaining
a certain gauge is not essential for this pattern.

ABBREVIATIONS
See page 120.

NOTE
The size may be adapted by using more or fewer chain at the
beginning, so long as the pattern is worked in multiples of 6 + 1,
and by working more or fewer rows.

TABLECLOTH
Ch 92.
Row 1: 1 sc in 2nd ch from hook, * skip 2 ch, 5 dc in next ch (shell made),
skip 2 ch, 1 sc in next ch, repeat from * ending with 1 sc in last ch, turn.

Row 2: Ch 3, 2 dc in first st (half shell) * 1 sc in center dc of shell on previous row, work 5 dc in next sc, repeat from * ending with 3 dc in last sc, turn.

Row 3: Ch 1, 1 sc in first dc * 5 dc in next sc, 1 sc in center dc of next shell, repeat from * ending with 1 sc in top 3 ch, turn.

Repeat rows 2 and 3 until 60 rows have been worked, placing dots as described below.

Fasten off.

Working the dots

Dots are worked in yarns B and C over 3 rows; pick up new color on last pull-through of previous stitch.

Row 1 of dot: Work a 5-dc shell.

Row 2 of dot: Work the 3 dc either side of shell on previous row.

Row 3 of dot: Work the 5-dc shell as above in row 1.

Place the dots as follows:

Rows 9, 29, and 49: Start the dot on the 4th, 8th, and 12th shells.

Rows 19 and 39: Start the dot on the 5th and 10th shells.

Alternate the colors of the dots on each row.

EDGING

Worked in yarn A all around the tablecloth, starting at one corner:
* 1 sc in edge, skip 2 sts, 5 dc in next st, skip 2 sts, repeat from * all around and sl st to join.

CROCHET BALLS (Make 4 in each color—12 in total)

Ch 3, join with sl st to form a ring.

Row 1: Ch 3, 12 dc into ring, join with sl st to top of ch-3.

Row 2: Ch 1, 1 sc in each st, sl st to join.

Rows 3 and 4: Repeat row 2.

Fasten off, leaving a tail of about 4 inches (10cm).

Using a tapestry needle, weave this tail through the tops of all the stitches on the last row.

Stuff ball with scraps of same color of yarn, insert weight into center, and draw up tightly.

FINISHING

To attach the balls, use yarn A to make 15 ch and fasten off, leaving a tail of about 4 inches (10cm).

Knot the 2 loose ends together to make a ring and tie securely to the loose end of the crochet ball. Conceal the loose ends inside the crochet ball. Repeat for the 11 other balls.

Attach the balls to the tablecloth (1 on each corner and 2 spaced equally along each side) by inserting the ch loop through the middle of an edge shell and pushing the crochet ball through the loop.

This amazing tent can be staked to the ground or slung over the branches of a tree to create a picnic "camp." Alternatively, suspend it on ropes over an outdoor dining table to make a gorgeous garden canopy. Decorate it with crocheted flowers or weave outdoor Christmas-tree lights through the net to make it even more magical and romantic.

Papillon Canopy   Leigh Radford

MATERIALS
Rowan Bamboo Tape (100% Bamboo, approx. 1¾ oz/50g, 82 yards/75m) in the following shades and quantities:
21 balls shade 711 Antique Rose (yarn A)
10 balls shade 705 Wafer (yarn B)
Sizes 4mm (F/5), 5mm (H/8) and 9mm (M/13) crochet hooks (see page 120)
Chenille needle (sharp point)
Approximately 80 feet (24.4m) of manila rope, ⅜ inch (1cm) thick

MEASUREMENTS
Approximately 10¼ feet (3.15m) long; 9½ feet (2.9m) wide.

GAUGE
Each mesh—from one knot to next, fully stretched—measures approximately 2¾ inches (7cm) using size 9mm (M/13) crochet hook, or the size required to obtain the correct gauge.

ABBREVIATIONS
See page 120.

SPECIAL ABBREVIATIONS
SK–Solomon's knot: See page 130.

MAIN PANELS (Make 5)
Using largest hook and yarn A, ch 1 drawing up loop to approximately 1¾ inches (4.5cm). Wrap the yarn over the hook, drawing the loop on the hook through, keeping the single back thread of this long chain separate from the 2 front threads. Insert the hook under this single back thread and wrap the yarn again. Draw a loop through and wrap again. Draw through both loops on the hook. Ch 1. One SK is completed. Repeat until you have completed 18 SK.

Row 1: Turn work and ch 1 in 3rd knot from hook drawing up loop to 1¾ inches (4.5cm). Repeat steps above, creating 2 SK. * Skip one knot from previous row and work 1 sc in next knot. Repeat from * across to end. Work 2 "end knots" drawing up loops only 1½ inches (3.5cm) instead of 1¾ inches (4.5cm).
Work all rows as for row 1, working even until panel measures approximately 124 inches (315cm) long.

DIVIDERS (Make 6)
Using medium-size hook and yarn B, ch 325.
Row 1: Change to smallest hook and beginning with 3rd ch from hook, work one dc in each ch to end of row (325 dc). Ch 2, turn.
Row 2: One dc in each dc of previous row to end. Fasten off. Darn in ends. (The dividers will be slightly shorter than the main panels.)

RINGS (Make 54)
Using medium-size hook and yarn B, ch 9. Insert hook into first ch and join with sl st.
Ch 1. Work 13 sc in center of ring. Insert hook into top of starting chain and make a sl st to join. Cut, leaving a tail of approximately 3 inches (7.5cm).

FINISHING

Lay all the main panels side by side on a flat surface, as shown in the diagram below. Lay one divider on top of the outside edge of the first main panel (slightly overlapping the edges). Pin one end of the divider to the top corner of the panel and pin the opposite end of the divider to the bottom corner of the panel, stretching the divider to fit. (Making the dividers shorter than the main panels and stretching them into place results in a sturdier piece of fabric, once the entire canopy has been assembled.) Pin the entire divider along the edge/length of the main panel.

Cut strand of yarn B 6½ yards (6m) long. Thread through chenille needle and pull flush with opposite end, dividing overall length to 3¼ yards (3m) (double strand). Beginning at lower right corner, Insert threaded needle into wrong side of divider and sew divider to panel, using whip stitch, removing pins as you work. Repeat for each panel until entire canopy is assembled. Working on wrong side of canopy, position rings at both ends of first divider and every 13¾ inches (35cm) in between (you will have nine rings per dividing panel). Thread 3-inch (7.5cm) tail from ring through needle and sew base of ring to divider, using whip stitch, until securely fastened.

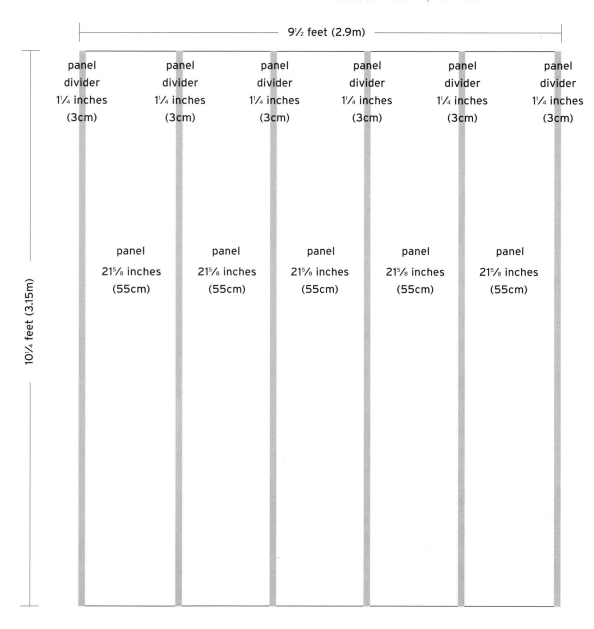

9½ feet (2.9m)

| panel divider 1¼ inches (3cm) | panel divider 1¼ inches (3cm) | panel divider 1¼ inches (3cm) | panel divider 1¼ inches (3cm) | panel divider 1¼ inches (3cm) | panel divider 1¼ inches (3cm) |

panel 21⅝ inches (55cm)　　panel 21⅝ inches (55cm)　　panel 21⅝ inches (55cm)　　panel 21⅝ inches (55cm)　　panel 21⅝ inches (55cm)

10¼ feet (3.15m)

Here is a great catch-all shoulder bag to carry your essentials, from magazine or book to sunglasses and water bottle—perfect for shopping, days out, picnics, or going to the beach. The mouthwatering burnt-orange yarn is like a burst of summer sunshine and will make you feel happy even if the sky is cloudy. Customize your bag by using some gorgeous wide ribbon for the shoulder strap.

Hipster Tote

Bee Clinch

MATERIALS
8 balls ggh Big Easy (worsted, 100% cotton, approx. 1¾ oz/50g, 75⅝ yards/70m), shade 3 Burnt Orange
Size 5mm (H/8) crochet hook (see page 120)
1 yard (1m) of fabric for lining
3¼ yards (3m) linen ribbon, 2 inches (5cm) wide
Tapestry needle
Sewing machine
Sewing needle
Matching sewing thread
Piece of strong cardboard, at least 12 x 3½ inches (30 x 9cm)

MEASUREMENTS
14 inches (36cm) deep x approximately 12 inches (30cm) wide at bottom.

GAUGE
13 sts to 4 inches (10cm) using 5mm (H/8) crochet hook, or the size required to obtain the correct gauge.

ABBREVIATIONS
See page 120.

SPECIAL ABBREVIATIONS

ps—puff stitch: Yarn over hook, insert into stitch and pull up loop (approximately ¾ inch [2cm]), yarn over hook, insert into same stitch and pull up loop to same length as previous. Repeat this process 4 times in total (9 loops), yarn over hook and pull through all loops on hook. Close puff stitch made with 1 chain.

sc into back loop: Sc in the usual way but into the back loop of the stitch only.

FRONT AND BASE

Ch 30 + 1.

Row 1: Sc into 2nd ch from hook. Sc to end. Ch 1, turn.

Row 2: Sc into back loop of next st, repeat to end. Ch 1, turn.

Repeat row 2 for 12 rows in total.

Proceed in puff-stitch pattern.

Row 1: Sc to end. Ch 2, turn.

Row 2: Ps into first st, repeat to end (30 ps in total). Ch 1, turn.

Repeat row 1 but sc only into top stitch of ps and not the stitch between. This sets the pattern.

Repeat rows 1 and 2 eleven times each.

Next row: Sc to end.

To form the base panel

Row 1: Sl st 3 st, sc to last 3 sts. 25 sts. Ch 1, turn.

Row 2: Sc into next sc 2 rows below. Continue sc into all stitches 2 rows below. Ch 1, turn.

Repeat rows 1 and 2 for 10 rows. Fasten off.

BACK

Complete as for front, omitting base panel.

FINISHING

Placing wrong sides together, match base panel to back piece, making sure that there is a 3-st difference to either side. Either sew the two pieces together or join with sc.

Sew or crochet the front and back side seams together along the ps rows and ridged top facing only, leaving the bottom seams open. Match the sewn side seam to center of base section and sew together. Complete for other side.

Reinforced base

Ch 40 + 1. Turn.

Row 1: Sc in 2nd ch from hook, sc to end. Ch 1, turn.

Continue in sc until piece measures 5½ in. (14cm). Fasten off.

Fold piece in half and sc tog around 2 sides.

Cut a piece of strong cardboard to fit inside and slip in. Sc closed and then place in bottom of bag to fit into base section.

Ribbon handle

Fold ribbon in half and adjust to length required. Sew together along both sides of ribbon. Sew each end securely at side seams at 2nd and 3rd ps rows.

Fabric lining

1. Cut two pieces of lining fabric, for front and back of bag, each measuring 15 x 17 inches (38 x 43cm) wide. Cut one piece of lining fabric for the base, measuring 13½ x 4½ inches (34 x 11cm).

2. Place the front and back panels together with right sides facing and machine stitch the side seams. Finish the raw edges with zigzag stitch or make a French seam to enclose raw edges. (To make a French seam, first sew the seam with wrong sides facing, trim and press, then sew the seam with right sides facing so the raw edges are enclosed.)

3. With right sides facing, insert the base panel, matching the sewn side seams to the center of the shorter sides of the base panel; pin then machine stitch. Finish raw edges as above.

4. Press under a ½-inch (1cm) hem along top edge. Turn lining right side out and press.

5. Place lining in crochet bag and slipstitch to inside of bag where ridged facing joins first ps row, being sure to cover ribbon ends.

Gorgeous Gifts

Made with pear tree's yummy ultra-soft merino yarn in colors that remind us of old-fashioned pajamas faded with wear, this beautiful blanket feels almost as good as cashmere. It makes the perfect gift for a newborn baby and is sure to be treasured for years to come. Or you may think it's so divine that you'll want to keep going and size it up for your own bed.

Baby Blanket of Roses

Kate Samphier

MATERIALS
pear tree 8-ply (Aran [worsted] weight) Merino (100% Australian
   merino wool, approx. 1¾ oz/50g, 107 yards/97.8m) in the following
   shades and quantities: 3 balls shade Moss, 1 ball in each of the
   following shades: Blush, Grass, Ecru, Robin's Egg
Size 5mm (H/8) crochet hook (see page 120)
Small pompom maker or cardboard to make pompom template
   (see page 136)
Tapestry needle

Color combination 1
Yarn A—Ecru
Yarn B—Robin's Egg
Yarn C—Moss

Color combination 2
Yarn A—Ecru
Yarn B—Blush
Yarn C—Moss

Double-knot stitch embroidery
Yarn D—Grass

MEASUREMENTS
Approximately 20 x 28 inches (50 x 70cm).

GAUGE
14 sts = 4 inches (10cm) over pattern worked with size 5mm (H/8)
crochet hook, or the size required to obtain the correct gauge.

ABBREVIATIONS
See page 120.

NOTE
By increasing the number of squares, you can increase the dimensions of your blanket.

BLANKET
Work a total of 15 squares: 8 in color combination 1 and 7 in color combination 2, as follows:

Base ring: Using yarn A, ch 12, join with sl st.
Round 1: Ch 1, 18 sc into ring, sl st to first sc. 18 sts.
Round 2: Ch 1, into same st as ch-1, * 1 sc, ch 3, skip 2 sts, repeat from * 6 times, sl st to first sc.
Round 3: Ch 1, work a petal of (1 sc, ch 3, 5 dc, ch 3, 1 sc) into each of 6 x ch-3 arches, sl st to first sc.
Round 4: Ch 1, (1 sc between 2 sc on round 3, ch 5 behind petal of 3rd round) 6 times, sl st to first sc.
Round 5: Ch 1, work a petal of (1 sc, ch 3, 7 dc, ch 3, 1 sc) into each of next 6 x ch arches, sl st to first sc.
Fasten off.

Round 6: Using yarn B join between 2 sc, ch 1, (1 sc between 2 sc on round 5, ch 6 behind petal of 5th round) 6 times, sl st to first sc.
Round 7: Sl st into next ch, ch 3 (count as 1 dc), * (4 dc, ch 2, 1 dc) all into same arch, 6 dc into next arch, (2 dc, ch 2, 4 dc) all into next arch ** 1 dc into next arch, rep from * to **, sl st to top of ch-3.
Round 8: Ch 3 (count as 1 dc), 1 dc into each dc all around with (3 dc, ch 2, 3 dc) into each ch-2 corner sp, ending sl st to top of ch-3.
Fasten off.

Round 9: Using yarn C join into same place, ch 1, 1 sc into same st as ch-1, * 1 sc into next st, work a ch-3 picot of (ch 3, sl st down through top of last sc made) twice, 1 sc into each of next 3 sts, work (ch-3 picot, 1 sc into next st) twice, (1 sc, ch 7, 1 sc) into corner ch-2 sp, (1 sc into next st, ch-3 picot) twice, 1 sc into each of next 3 sts, (ch-3 picot, 1 sc into next st) twice, 1 sc into next st, rep from * 3 times omitting sc at end of last rep, sl st to first sc.
Round 10: Sl st across to top of next ch-3 picot, ch 1, 1 sc into same picot, * ch 5, skip next picot, 1 sc into next picot, ch 5, (1 sc, ch 7, 1 sc) into corner ch-7 arch (ch 5, skip next picot, 1 sc into next picot) twice, ch 5, 1 sc into next picot; rep from * 3 times omitting sc at end of last rep, sl st to first sc.
Fasten off.

FINISHING
Lightly press each square, referring to the ball band (see page 137).

Overcast the squares together, alternating the two colorways to create a patchwork grid of 5 squares by 3 squares.

Double-knot embroidery
With right side facing, work double-knot embroidery stitch along each seam in yarn D (see page 135).

Edging
With right side facing, work 1 row of dc in yarn C along the side edges of blanket, working into every alternate stitch.

Change to yarn D, and work picot edge all around blanket:
Working into loops from previous row, * ch 3, 1 sc in first of these ch, skip 1 st, 1 sc in next st; rep from * to end. Fasten off.

Make 4 pompoms in yarn B (in your preferred colorway) (see page 136) of approx. 1¾ inches (4.5cm) diameter and sew one to each corner of the blanket.

The nostalgic appeal of this cute little cardigan is undeniable—from the soft mauve color to the pretty shape and the flower-shaped buttons. Alicia Paulson dreams of a place in the Midwest where the summers seem impossibly long, where the beds are dressed in crisp white cotton, where a neighbor's porch swing rocks gently in the breeze and the lightning bugs hover. Making this baby's cardigan gives you a little taste of that magical place.

"Maisie" Cardigan Alicia Paulson

MATERIALS

5 (5, 6) balls Debbie Bliss Baby Cashmerino (worsted, 55% merino wool, 33% microfiber, 12% Cashmere, approx. 1¾ oz/50g, 136¾ yards/125m), shade 608 Mauve

Sizes 3mm (C/2½) and 4mm (G/6) crochet hooks (see page 120)

3 buttons, approx. ½ inch (1cm) diameter

Tapestry needle

MEASUREMENTS

To fit age: 3-6 months (6-12 months, 12-24 months).

Finished chest measurement: 18(20, 22) inches (45[50, 55]cm).

NOTE

Instructions for larger sizes are given in parentheses. Where there is only one figure, it applies to all sizes.

GAUGE

20 sts and 15 rows to 4 inches (10cm) over yoke-pattern stitch, using size 3mm (C/2½) crochet hook or the size required to obtain the correct gauge.

ABBREVIATIONS

See page 120.

BACK YOKE

Using smaller hook, ch 50 (54, 58).

Row 1 (RS): Hdc in 3rd ch from hook and in each ch across to end; turn. 48 (52, 56) sts.

Row 2: Ch 2, hdc in each st across to end; turn.

Armhole shaping

Row 1: Ch 2, hdc2tog (dec made); pattern across to last 2 sts, hdc2tog; turn. 46 (50, 54) sts.

Rows 2-5: Repeat row 1. 38 (42, 46) sts after row 5.

Row 6: Ch 2, hdc in each st across to end; turn.

Repeat row 6 until back measures approx. 4 (4½, 5) inches (10 [11.5, 13]cm from beginning, ending with a WS row. Fasten off.

LEFT FRONT YOKE

Using smaller hook, ch 26 (28, 30).

Row 1 (RS): Hdc in 3rd ch from hook and in each ch across to end; turn. 24 (26, 28) sts.

Row 2: Ch 2, hdc in each st across to end; turn.

Left front armhole shaping

Row 1: Ch 2, hdc2tog (dec made); hdc in each st across to end; turn. 23 (25, 27) sts.

Row 2: Ch 2, hdc in each st across to last 2 sts, hdc2tog; turn. 22 (24, 26) sts.

Rows 3-5: Repeat rows 1 and 2. 19 (21, 23) sts after row 5.

Row 6: Ch 2, hdc in each st across; turn.

Repeat row 6 until Left Front measures approx. 2½ (3, 3½) inches (6 [8, 9]cm from beginning, ending with a WS row.

Left front neck shaping

Row 1 (RS): Ch 2, hdc in each st across, leaving last 8 (10, 10) sts unworked; turn. 11 (11, 13) sts.

Row 2: Ch 2, hdc2tog, hdc in each st across to end; turn. 10 (10, 12) sts.

Row 3: Ch 2, hdc in each st across to last 2 sts, hdc2tog; turn. 9 (9, 11) sts.

Row 4: Ch 2, hdc in each st across to end; turn.

Repeat row 4 until Left Front measures 4 (4½, 5) inches (10 [11.5, 13]cm) from beginning. Fasten off.

RIGHT FRONT YOKE

Make as for Left Front, reversing armhole and neck shaping.

Note: For neck shaping, on RS row sl st in first 8 (10, 10) sts then continue pattern across. Complete as for Left Front.

SLEEVES

Using smaller hook, ch 28 (30, 32).

Row 1 (RS): Hdc in 3rd ch from hook, hdc in next 10 (11, 12) ch, 2 hdc in next 6 ch, hdc in next 10 (11, 12) ch; turn. 32 (34, 36) sts.

Row 2: Ch 2, 2 hdc in first st, hdc in each st across to last st, 2 hdc in last st; turn. 34 (36, 38) sts.

Rows 3–5: Repeat row 2 three more times; turn. 40 (42, 44) sts.

Row 6: Ch 2, hdc in each st across to end; turn.

Repeat row 6 until sleeve measures 3¼ (3¾, 4¼) inches (8 [9.5, 11]cm).

Sleeve edging

Row 1: Ch 2, hdc in next st, (hdc in next 5 sts, hdc2tog in next st) 6 times, hdc in last hdc; turn. 34 (36, 38) sts.

Row 2: Ch 2, skip first st, dc in next st, sc in previous st, (skip next st, dc in next st, sc in previous st) across to end; turn.

Row 3: Ch 1, sc.in each st across to end. Fasten off.

LOWER PART OF CARDIGAN

With wrong sides facing, sew Right Front and Left Front to Back at shoulders. Sew sleeves into armholes; gather and ease around top if necessary. Sew up side and underarm seams.

With RS facing and using larger hook, join yarn at bottom edge of Left Front.

Row 1: Ch 1, working in bottom loops of foundation chain, (sc in next st, 2 sc in next st) across to end. 144 (156, 168) sts.

Row 2: Ch 2, skip first st, dc in next st, sc in previous st. (Skip next st, dc in next st, sc in previous st) across to end; turn.

Repeat row 2 until bodice measures 9½ (10½, 11½) inches (24 [27, 29]cm) from shoulder, ending with a WS row; turn.

Next Row: Ch 1, sc in each st across to end. Fasten off.

TRIM

With RS facing and using smaller hook, join yarn with sl st at lower edge of Right Front Yoke.

Ch 5 (or as many as necessary to go around button) to form loop for button, sc evenly halfway up yoke, ch 5 to form loop for button, sc evenly up to top of yoke, ch 5 to form loop for button, sc in same st twice to turn corner.

Sc evenly around neck edge and down front of yoke, making 3 sc in last st of Right Front to turn corner.

Fasten off.

FINISHING

Darn in all ends and block lightly (see page 137).

Sew buttons to yoke approx. 1¼ inches (3cm) apart, directly opposite button loops.

Syd has been lovingly designed to appeal to children of all ages—even adult ones. He can be played with and loved by little ones, or sit on a chair or bed to keep more mature "children" in touch with their childhood. Syd has a somewhat motley construction, and the handmade quality means that whoever crochets this rabbit will make him slightly different, giving him a unique character.

"Syd" Rabbit   Claire Montgomerie

MATERIALS

2 balls Blue Sky Alpacas Melange (DK, 100% alpaca, approx. 1¾ oz/50g, 109⅜ yards/100m), shade 805 Huckleberry (yarn A)

1 ball Blue Sky Alpacas Sportweight (100% baby alpaca, approx. 1¾ oz/ 50g, 109⅜ yards/100m) in each of the following shades: 30 Blue Sky (yarn B), 517 Lemondrop (yarn C), 506 Natural Streaky Brown (or any scraps of yarn for embroidering face and finishing touches) (yarn D)

Sizes 4mm (G/6) and 2.5mm (B/1½) crochet hooks

Toy stuffing, such as polyester fiberfill

Tapestry needle

Small pompom maker or carboard to make template (see page 136)

MEASUREMENTS

Length (from top of head to feet): 15 inches (38cm).
Length (from top of head to bottom of body): 10½ inches (27cm).
Belly circumference (at widest): 12½ inches (32cm).
Span of arms (opened wide): 15 inches (38cm).

GAUGE

Obtaining a certain gauge is not essential, but when making toys, make sure that you crochet tightly; otherwise the stuffing will show through the gaps. This means that you may have to use a hook that you would usually consider much too small for your yarn.

ABBREVIATIONS

See page 120.

SPECIAL ABBREVIATIONS

dec—decrease 1 by working 2 sts together.

BODY

Begin stuffing the body when you start to decrease for the neck. It will be easier than stuffing when the body is finished.

Using larger hook and yarn A, ch 3, 8 sc in 2nd ch from hook, join round with sl st.

Round 1: Ch 1, 1 sc into same st, * 2 sc in next st, rep from * to end, join round with sl st. 16 sts.

Round 2: Ch 1, 2 sc in next st, * 1 sc in next st, 2 sc in next st, rep from * to end, join round with sl st. 24 sts.

Round 3: Ch 1, 2 sc in next st, * 1 sc in next st, 2 sc in next st, rep from * to end, join round with sl st. 36 sts.

Round 4: Ch 1, 1 sc in next st, 2 sc into next st, * 2 sc, 2 sc into next st, rep from * to end, join round with sl st. 48 sts.

Round 5: Ch 1, 1 sc in each st all around. 48 sts.

Round 6: Ch 1, 2 sc, 2 sc into next st, * 3 sc, 2 sc into next st, rep from * to end, join round with sl st. 60 sts.

Round 7: Ch 1, work 1 sc in each st all around. 60 sts.

Round 8: Ch 1, 3 sc, 2 sc into next st, * 4 sc, 2 sc into next st, rep from * to end, join round with sl st. 72 sts.

Round 9: Sl st all around, working through back loop of each st only. 72 sts.

Work 3 rounds straight in sc. 72 sts.

Round 13: Ch 1, 4 sc, 2 sc into next st, * 5 sc, 2 sc into next st, rep from * to end, join round with sl st. 84 sts.

Work 4 rounds straight in sc. 84 sts.

Round 18: Ch 1, 4 sc, dec 1 st, * 5 sc, dec 1 st, rep from * to end, join round with sl st. 72 sts.

Work 4 rounds straight in sc. 72 sts.

Round 23: Ch 1, 3 sc, dec 1 st, * 4 sc, dec 1 st, rep from * to end, join round with sl st. 60 sts.

Work 6 rounds straight in sc. 60 sts.

Round 30: Ch 1, 2 sc, dec 1 st, * 3 sc, dec 1 st, rep from * to end, join round with sl st. 48 sts.

Work 4 rounds straight in sc. 48 sts.

Round 35: Ch 1, 1 sc, dec 1 st, * 2 sc, dec 1 st, rep from * to end, join round with sl st. 36 sts.

Work straight for 6 rows in sc. (36 sts).

Round 42: Dec all around. 18 sts.

Work 1 row straight in sc.

Round 44: Dec all around. 9 sts.

Fasten off yarn.

HEAD

Using larger hook and yarn A, ch 3, 6 sc in 2nd ch from hook, join round with sl st.

Round 1: Ch 1, 1 sc into same st, * 2 sc in next st, rep from * to end, join round with sl st. 12 sts.

Round 2: Ch 1, 2 sc in next st, * 1 sc in next st, 2 sc in next st, rep from * to end, join round with sl st. 18 sts.

Round 3: Ch 1, 3 sc in next st, * 1 sc in next st, 3 sc in next st, rep from * to end, join round with sl st. 24 sts.

Work 1 round straight in sc. 24 sts.

Round 5: Ch 1, 2 sc, 2 sc into next st, * 3 sc, 2 sc into next st, rep from * to end, join round with sl st. 30 sts.

Work 1 round straight in sc. 30 sts.

Round 7: Ch 1, 3 sc, 2 sc into next st, * 4 sc, 2 sc into next st, rep from * to end, join round with sl st. 36 sts.

Work 1 round straight in sc. 36 sts.

Round 9: Ch 1, 4 sc, 2 sc into next st, * 5 sc, 2 sc into next st, rep from * to end, join round with sl st. 42 sts.

Work 4 rows straight in sc. 42 sts.

Round 14: Ch 1, 4 sc, dec 1 st, * 5 sc, dec 1 st, rep from * to end, join round with sl st. 36 sts.

Work 1 row straight in sc. 36 sts.

Round 16: Ch 1, 3 sc, dec 1 st, * 4 sc, dec 1 st, rep from * to end, join round with sl st. 30 sts.

Work 1 row straight in sc. 30 sts.

Round 18: Ch 1, 2 sc, dec 1 st, * 3 sc, dec 1 st, rep from * to end, join round with sl st. 24 sts.

Round 19: Ch 1, 1 sc, dec 1 st, * 2 sc, dec 1 st, rep from * to end, join round with sl st. 18 sts.

Fasten off yarn.

Stuff head with toy filling and sew to top of body, making sure that each part is filled sufficiently so that the head does not flop over.

ARMS

Using larger hook and yarn A, ch 3, 5 sc in 2nd ch from hook, join round with sl st.

Round 1: Ch 1, 1 sc into same st, * 2 sc in next st, rep from * to end, join round with sl st. 10 sts.

Round 2: Ch 1, 2 sc in next st, * 1 sc in next st, 2 sc in next st, rep from * to end, join round with sl st. 15 sts.

Round 3: Work round in sc.

Work as round 3 until arm measures approx. 6½ inches (16cm), beginning stuffing halfway through, as this will be easier than stuffing at the end.

Fasten off yarn.

Make another arm in the same way and sew each to body.

LEGS

Using larger hook and yarn A, ch 3, 5 sc in 2nd ch from hook, join round with sl st.

Round 1: Ch 1, 1 sc into same st, * 2 sc in next st, rep from * to end, join round with sl st. 10 sts.

Round 2: Work round in sc.

Work as round 2 until leg measures approx. 2½ inches (6cm).

Fasten off yarn.

Make another leg in the same way.

FEET

Using larger hook and yarn A, ch 3, 6 sc in 2nd ch from hook, join round with sl st.

Round 1: Ch 1, 1 sc into same st, * 2 sc in next st, rep from * to end, join round with sl st. 12 sts.

Round 2: Ch 1, sc in first sc, hdc in each of next 2 sc, 3 dc in next sc, hdc in each of next 2 sc, sc in next sc, hdc in each of next 2 sc, 3 dc in next sc, sc to end of round, sl st to join round. 16 sts.

Round 3: Ch 1, sc to center st of 3-dc inc of previous round, 4 sc, 1 hdc, 2 dc into next st, 3 dc into next st, 2 dc into next st, 1 hdc, sc to end of round, join round with sl st. 20 sts.

Round 4: Ch 1, sc to center st of 3-sc inc of previous round, 3 sc into next st, sc to 1 st before hdc of previous round, hdc into sc, dc into hdc, 2 dc into next dc, 2 dtr (yarn over hook twice) into dc, 2 dc into next st, 3 dc into central st, 2 dc into next st, 2 dtr into next st, 2 dc into next st, dc, hdc, sc to end of round, sl st to join round. 30 sts.

Round 5: Ch 1, sc to center inc st of previous round, 3 sc into next st, sc to first hdc of previous round, hdc, dc, 2 dc into next st, 2 dc into next st, 2 dtr into next st, dc into each st across, to 2nd dtr of previous round, 2 dtr into next st, 2 dc into next st, 2 dc into next st, dc, hdc, sc to end of round, join with sl st. 38 sts.

Fasten off yarn.

Make another foot in yarn A and one each of yarns B and C.

Sew one yarn A and one yarn C foot piece together and stuff. Repeat with remaining two foot pieces in yarn A and yarn B. With yarn A side on top and the other color for the sole, sew a foot to each leg and stuff the legs. Sew each leg to body.

Sew tummy in place on body. Add a row of blanket stitch around the edge if desired (see page 134).

EARS

Left ear
Using larger hook and yarn A, ch 19.

Row 1: Work 1 hdc into 3rd ch from hook, work 1 dc into each ch to end, working only through one loop, in end ch work 3 dc, and continue along other side of chain, working 1 dc in each ch to end, working through remaining loop of each ch. Ch 3, turn. 39 sts.

Row 2: Work as row 1, but working through both loops of each st.

Row 3: Work in dc to 3 sts from end st, work 1 hdc into next st, dc, 3 trtr into end st, dc, hdc, dc to end of round.

Fasten off yarn.

Work another ear piece in yarn B. Sew two ear pieces together, fold in half and sew together along bottom. Attach to head.

Right ear
Using larger hook and yarn A, ch 23.

Row 1: Work 1 hdc into 3rd ch from hook, work 1 dc into each ch to end, working through only one loop, in end ch work 3 dc, and continue along other side of chain, working 1 dc in each ch to end, working through rem loop of each ch. Ch 3, turn. 39 sts.

Rows 2 and 3: Work 2 more rows in this way, but working through both loops of each st.

Fasten off yarn.

Work another ear piece in yarn C. Sew two ear pieces together, fold in half and sew together along bottom. Attach to head.

FINISHING
Embroider face and extra embellishments as desired in Yarn D or scraps of leftover yarn.

Make two eyes using smaller hook and yarn B as follows:
Ch 3, 4 sc in 2nd ch from hook, join round with sl st.

Round 1: Ch 1, sc into same st, 2 sc into each st around. 8 sts. Fasten off yarn.

If you wish, you can make the next eye bigger by adding one more round in the same way as round 1.

Sew eyes to head.

For the tail, make a pompom approx. 1¾ inches (4.5cm) in diameter (see page 136), using one or an assortment of the yarns. Sew the tail in place at the bottom rear of the body.

TUMMY
Using larger hook and yarn C, ch 3, 6 sc in 2nd ch from hook, join round with sl st.

Round 1: Ch 1, 1 sc into same st, * 2 sc in next st, rep from * to end, join round with sl st. 12 sts.

Round 2: Ch 1, 2 sc in next st, * 1 sc in next st, 2 sc in next st, rep from * to end, join round with sl st. 18 sts.

Round 3: Ch 1, 3 sc in next st, * 1 sc in next st, 3 sc in next st, rep from * to end, join round with sl st. 24 sts.

Round 4: Ch 1, 2 sc, 2 sc into next st, * 3 sc, 2 sc into next st, rep from * to end, join round with sl st. 30 sts.

Round 5: Ch 1, 3 sc, 2 sc into next st, * 4 sc, 2 sc into next st, rep from * to end, join round with sl st. 36 sts.

Round 6: Ch 3, 4 dc, 2 dc into next st, * 5 dc, 2 dc into next st, rep from * to end, join round with sl st. 42 sts.

Round 7: Ch 3, 5 dc, 2 dc into next st, * 6 dc, 2 dc into next st, rep from * to end, join round with sl st. 48 sts.

Round 8: Ch 3, 6 dc, 2 dc into next st, * 7 dc, 2 dc into next st, rep from * to end, join round with sl st. 54 sts.

Fasten off yarn.

This traditional "clasp" purse adds a touch of elegance to any outfit and is just the right size to hold money, compact, and lipstick—which makes it ideal for parties or weddings. The berry-colored yarn is offset by the vintage floral lining.

Butterfly-Stitch Purse   Kate Samphier

MATERIALS

1 ball ggh Bel Air (worsted, 90% merino extra-fine, 10% polyamide, approx. 1¾ oz/50g, 142¼ yards/130m), shade 3 Deep Plum
Size 5mm (H/8) crochet hook (see page 120)
¼ yard (30cm) fabric for lining backing (bottle-green pinwale corduroy)
¼ yard (30cm) fabric for inner lining (floral linen)
One medium-sized silver purse frame
Sewing needle and thread
Fabric glue

MEASUREMENTS

Approximately 4 x 6½ inches (10 x 16cm).

GAUGE

I motif = approximately 1½ inches (3.5cm).
Obtaining a certain gauge is not essential.

ABBREVIATIONS

See page 120.

PURSE

Make 2 purse panels as follows.
Ch 31.
Row 1: Ch 3, then work in dc to end of row.
Row 2: Ch 3, 1 dc in 2nd dc, * skip 2 sts, 3 dc in next st, skip 2 sts, (1 dc, ch 3, 1 dc) in next st *, repeat from * 3 times, skip 2 sts, 2 dc in last st.
Row 3: Ch 3, 2 dc in ch-3 sp of previous row, * 1 sc in 2nd of 3 dc of previous row, 7 dc in next ch-3 sp *, repeat from * and finish with 3 dc in last ch-3 sp instead of 7 dc.
Row 4: Ch 3, 1 dc in first dc, * 3 dc in sc of previous row, (1 dc, ch 3, 1 dc) in 4th dc of group of 7 dc *.
Row 5: Repeat row 3.
Row 6: Repeat row 4.

Decrease

Row 7: Sc into 3rd dc, * 7 dc in ch-3 sp, 1 sc in 2nd of 3 dc of previous row, * sc.
Row 8: Ch 3, * 1 dc, ch 3, 1 dc in 4th of previous 7 dc, 3 dc into sc, * sc in 4th st of previous 7.
Row 9: Sc into 3 dc, * 7 dc in ch-3 sp, 1 sc in 2nd of 3 dc of previous row, * skip 1 st, sc.
Row 10: Ch 3, (1 dc, ch 3, 1 dc) into 4th of 7 dc, 3 dc of sc, (1 dc, 3 dc, 1 dc), into 4th of 7 dc, ch 3, skip 3 st sc. Fasten off.

FINISHING

1. Using the purse frame and the completed crochet panel, draw a template from which to cut the linings, allowing at least ½ inch (1cm) all around for seams and extra fabric at the hinge point to allow the purse to open. Cut 2 pieces of lining material and two pieces of backing material.
2. Baste backing fabric to wrong side of crochet panels.
3. Using a needle and thread, sew crochet panels to backing fabric.
4. With crochet sides facing each other, sew seams together from hinge point, down side, across bottom and up to other hinge point. Turn purse crochet side out.
5. With right sides together, sew bottom parts of inner lining fabric from hinge point, down side, across bottom and up to other hinge point. Finish raw edge with zigzag stitch or make a French seam (see page 91).
6. Place lining in crochet bag. Turn the edges in, adjusting the top of lining to fit purse.
7. On each side of purse, slipstitch top part of lining, with raw edges turned under, to top part of crochet, beginning where stitching stops at the hinge. Press if necessary.
8. Following the manufacturer's instructions, apply glue generously to one side of purse frame and to top and side edges of fabric around one side of purse opening. Allow glue to dry for 5 minutes, or as recommended.
9. Insert one side of purse into frame, starting at the hinge and working around the top and down the other side. Check that the lining is also inserted evenly. Allow glue to dry for 15 minutes, then glue the other side of the purse fabric into the frame in the same way.

Show your favorite furry friend how much you love him by making him this cozy sweater-coat. It'll keep him toasty on snowy winter days or brisk early morning walks, but it's comfortable to wear so it won't stop him from having fun chasing sticks, balls, other dogs—or his own tail. The "hoodie" design, complete with jaunty pompom, means he won't loose his street-cred, either; he'll still be the smartest dog on the block—and in the park.

"Woody" Dog Coat

Bee Clinch

MATERIALS
3 balls Lana Grossa Royal Tweed (chunky, 100% merino fine, approx.
   1¾ oz/50g, 109⅜ yards/100m), shade 36 Pink (yarn A)
1 ball Rowan Cashsoft (DK, 57% extra-fine merino, 33% microfiber,
   10% cashmere, approx. 1¾ oz/50g, 142¼ yards/130m), shade 509
   Lime (yarn B)
Size 5mm (H/8) crochet hook
Tapestry needle
4 vintage buttons, approx. ¾ inch (2cm) diameter
Small pompom maker or stiff cardboard to make pompom
   template (see page 136)

SIZE
To fit a small dog, such as a terrier, poodle, or small spaniel.
Length: From shoulder seam to bottom edge of back, approximately
12 inches (30cm).
Hood: From tip of hood to shoulder seam, approximately 7 inches
(18cm).
Chest circumference: Approximately 18½ inches (47cm).

GAUGE
12 sts to 4 inches (10cm), using size 5mm (H/8) crochet hook or the
size required to obtain correct gauge.

ABBREVIATIONS
See page 120.

SPECIAL ABBREVIATIONS

ps – puff stitch: To make a puff stitch of 4 half double crochet stitches, wrap yarn over hook, insert hook into stitch, wrap yarn again and draw a loop through (3 loops on hook). Repeat this step three more times, inserting the hook into the same stitch each time (9 loops on hook), wrap yarn and draw through all loops on hook. (See also page 123, where this stitch is shown worked in an openwork fabric.)

NOTE

This coat, with the cute pompom hood, has been specially designed for a pampered little dog, Woody. Small dogs normally feel the cold more than bigger dogs, unless it's exceptionally cold. But even then, a larger dog would look better in a simpler sweater, without a hood!

BACK

Using Yarn A ch 37 + 2. Turn.

Row 1: Sc into 2nd ch from hook, (1 sc, ch 1, skip next st for buttonhole) continue in sc to end, ch 1, turn.

Row 2: Sc into first st, ps into ch sp, sc, * ps, sc; repeat from *, ch 1, turn.

Row 3: As row 1, omitting buttonhole.

Every alternate row will follow this pattern.

Row 4: Sc into first st, * sc, ps, sc, repeat from * to last stitch, sc, ch 1, turn.

Row 6: 1 sc, * ps, 1 sc, repeat from * 3 times, sc to last 6 sts, repeat from * to end, ch 1, turn.

Row 8: 1 sc, * sc, ps, repeat from * 3 times, sc to last 7 sts, repeat from * to last st, sc, ch 1, turn.

Repeat this last 4-row pattern until the work measures 4 inches (10cm), finishing with a row 8.

As row 1, including buttonhole.

Next row: As row 6, but first ps will be in the first ch sp.

Continue in pattern until work measures 7½ inches (19cm).

Shaping

Row 1: Sl st 1, ch 1, sc to end, ch 1, turn.

Row 2: Sl st 1, ch 2, * ps, sc, repeat 4 times, sc to last 8 sts, repeat from * to end, ch 1, turn.

Repeat rows 1 and 2 four more times (10 rows in total). Finish with 2nd shaping row.

Final row: Sc, ch 1, skip st, (buttonhole), sc to end. Fasten off.

FRONT

Ch 14 + 1.

Next and continuing rows: Sc into 2nd ch from hook, sc to end. Ch 1, turn.

Continue in pattern until work measures 7½ inches (19cm).

Next row: Sl st 1, ch 1, sc to end.

Repeat this row 12 times in total. Fasten off.

HOOD

Ch 30 + 1.

Row 1: Sc in 2nd ch from hook, sc to end, ch 1, turn.

Row 2: Sc 1, * ps, sc, repeat from * to end, ch 1, turn.

Repeat row 1, omitting buttonhole (12 rows in total). Fasten off.

FINISHING

Placing wrong sides together, work sc along long side of Back (without buttonholes) and Front pieces to join.

Join firmly at neck opposite buttonhole.

Sew buttons on Front piece to match buttonholes on left side of Front.

Folding hood in half along long edge with wrong sides together, sc along one side.

Match center seam of Hood to center of Back and pin.

Join hood and body with sc.

Using yarn B, make a pompom of approx. 1¾ inches (4.5cm) diameter (see page 136) and sew onto top point of hood.

Now, walk the dawg!

Far too pretty to hide away in a closet, this lovely padded hanger would make a great gift for anyone from your grandma to your teenage sister. Covered in the softest fluffy yarn, it will be far kinder to delicate dresses or knits than a standard hanger, and will look so much more stylish. To make it even more special, embellish it with ribbon, beads, sequins, or buttons, then use it to display a favorite dress.

Hanger with Flowers Bee Clinch

MATERIALS

1 ball ggh Amelie (bulky, 100% polyamide [microfiber], approx. 1¾ oz/50g, 71 yards/65m), shade 12 Soft Blue (yarn A)
1 ball Jaeger Siena 4-Ply Cotton (sportweight, 100% mercerised cotton, approx. 1¾ oz/50g, 153⅛ yards/140m) in the following shades: 404 Lavender (yarn B), 405 Seaspray (yarn C)
Sizes 3mm (C/2½) and 6mm (J/10) crochet hooks (see page 120)
Padded hanger, 12½ inches (32cm) long (alternatively, use a wooden or plastic hanger and cover it with batting yourself)
5 small vintage buttons, approx. ½ inch (1cm) diameter
Tapestry needle
Small amount of fabric glue

MEASUREMENTS

Length of hanger: 12½ inches (32cm).
Diameter of flowers: Approximately 2 inches (5cm).

GAUGE

12 sts to 4 inches (10cm) over sc, using size 6mm (J/10) hook or the size required to obtain the correct gauge.

ABBREVIATIONS

See page 120.

NOTE

If your hanger is a different length, use the gauge to estimate how many chain to make.

HANGER COVER

Using larger hook and yarn A, ch 40 + 1 (for hanger measuring 12½ inches [32cm]).
Row 1: Sc into 2nd ch from hook, sc to end, ch 1, turn.
Row 2: Sc into first st, sc to end.
Repeat row 1 until 7 rows are completed. Fasten off.

FLOWER CASCADE

Using smaller hook and yarn B, ch 4. Sl st into first ch to form ring.
Round 1: * Ch 4, into ring work 3 dtr (yarn over hook 3 times), ch 4, sl st into circle. * Repeat from * to * 4 more times (5 petals in total).
Ch 40 after last sl st, ch 4, sl st into 4th ch from hook to form circle.
Repeat from * to * 5 times to create another 5-petal flower.
After last sl st, continue to sl st along 40-ch length to first flower.
Sl st into back of flower. Fasten off.
Make another cascade set, as above, using Yarn C.
Make one flower using Yarn B omitting sl-st cord.

FINISHING

Using tapestry needle, darn in all yarn ends.
Fold hanger cover in half with wrong sides together and close seams with sc, leaving a 5-inch (13cm) opening at the top. Insert hanger and close opening using tapestry needle and yarn.
Gently press flowers (referring to yarn labels).
Using yarn B or yarn C as appropriate, sew a button to the center of each flower.
Work metal hook of hanger through the slip-stitch cord between flowers, adjusting lengths as preferred.
Bind a long length of yarn C around metal hook, pushing down flower cords close to base. Finish binding at tip of hook, and dab a small amount of glue to fix.
Glue the single yarn B flower to the base of the hook.

Add instant panache to any item in your wardrobe with this gorgeous peony corsage—a simple way to embellish clothes and give them a fresh new look. Whether you use it to dress up a cardigan, jacket, or coat lapel, or pin it onto a bag, this blowsy bloom will give the garment a pretty, feminine touch.

Peony Corsage   Kate Jenkins

MATERIALS

1 ball ggh Bel Air (worsted, 90% merino extra-fine, 10% polyamide, approx. 1¾ oz/50g, 142¼ yards/130m) in each of the following shades: 1 Pink (yarn A), 2 Lilac (yarn B), 3 Deep Plum (yarn C), 20 Dark Olive (yarn D), 21 Pale Olive (yarn E)
Size 4.5mm (G/7) crochet hook (see page 120)
Batting or scraps of yarn to stuff bobble
Tapestry needle

MEASUREMENTS

Central bobble: Approximately 2 inches (5cm) diameter.
Inner petals: Approximately 4¾ inches (12cm) diameter.
Outer petals: Approximately 5½ inches (14cm) diameter.
Leaves: 2 inches (5cm) long, 2 inches (5cm) at widest point.

GAUGE

Obtaining a certain gauge is not essential; however, it should be fairly tight—especially for the bobble, so the stuffing does not show through.

ABBREVIATIONS

See page 120.

NOTE

If you wish to add more color detail to the petals, work around the edges in picot crochet (ch 3, 1 sl st) using an additional contrasting color.

BOBBLE

Using yarn A, ch 6, sl st into first chain to form ring.
Round 1: Ch 3, 20 dc, sl st into top of ch-3.
Round 2: Ch 3, 1 dc into each dc of previous round, sl st into top of ch-3.
Round 3: Repeat round 2.
Round 4: Ch 3, work 2 dc tog (repeat 10 times), sl st into top of ch-3. At this stage, start to fill bobble with stuffing (batting or yarn scraps).
Round 5: * Ch 2, work 2 sc tog, repeat from * 5 times.

Fasten off and sew in ends.

INNER PETALS (Make 5 in yarn A and 5 in yarn B)

Row 1: Ch 5, skip 1 ch, 1 dc into next 4 ch, ch 1, turn.
Row 2: 2 dc into first dc, 1 dc into each of next 3 dc, 2 dc into last dc, ch 1, turn.
Row 3: 2 dc into first dc, 1 dc into next 4 dc, 2 dc into last dc, ch 1, turn.
Row 4: 2 dc into first dc, 1 dc into next 6 dc, 2 dc into last dc, ch 1, turn.
Row 5: Work 3 dc tog, 1 dc into next 4 dc, work 3 dc tog.
Fasten off and sew in ends.

OUTER PETALS (Make 5 in Yarn C)

Row 1: Ch 7, skip 1 ch, 1 dc into next 6 ch, ch 1, turn.
Row 2: 2 dc into next dc, 1 dc into next 4 dc, 2 dc into last dc, ch 1, turn.
Row 3: 2 dc into first dc, 1 dc into next 6 dc, 2 dc into last dc, ch 1, turn.
Row 4: 2 dc into next dc, 1 dc into next 8 dc, 2 dc into last dc, ch 1, turn.
Row 5: 2 dc into next dc, 1 dc into next 10 dc, 2 dc into last dc, ch 1, turn.
Row 6: Work 3 dc tog, 1 dc into next 8 dc, work 3 dc tog.
Fasten off and sew in ends.
When all petals are complete, sew onto bobble, starting with inner petals.

LEAF (Make 2 in yarn D)

Row 1: Ch 4, skip 1 ch, 3 dc into next 3 ch, ch 1, turn.
Row 2: 2 dc into first dc, 1 dc, 2 dc into last dc, ch 1, turn.
Row 3: 2 dc into first dc, 1 dc into next 3 dc, 2 dc into last dc, ch 1, turn.
Row 4: 2 dc into first dc, 1 dc into next 5 dc, 2 dc into last dc, ch 1, turn.
Row 5: 2 dc into first dc, 1 dc into next 7 dc, 2 dc into last dc, ch 1, turn.
Row 6: Work 2 dc tog, 1 dc into next 7 dc, work 2 dc tog, ch 1, turn.
Row 7: Work 2 dc tog, 1 dc into next 5 dc, work 2 dc tog, ch 1, turn.
Row 8: Work 2 dc tog, 1 dc into next 5 dc, work 2 dc tog, ch 1, turn.
Row 9: Work 2 dc tog, 1 dc into next 3 dc, work 2 dc tog, ch 1, turn.
Row 10: Work 3 dc tog, and fasten off.
Change to yarn E and join to bottom of leaf; work 2 rounds of dc into edge of leaf. Fasten off and sew in ends.
Using a tapestry needle and yarn E embroider vein details on leaves.

Appealingly tactile, the wonderful raised bobble stitch in an off-white yarn makes this the perfect summer handbag to complement anything from a jeans-and-T shirt combo to a fifties floral prom dress. Designed in a classic purse shape with chunky wooden handles, it's roomy enough for all your everyday essentials but not so outsize as to be cumbersome. Alternatively, you could use it for your crochet, knitting, or sewing kit. Cut up a favorite old summer dress to make a colorful and pretty lining.

Bobble-Stitch Handbag

Kate Jenkins

MATERIALS
10 balls ggh Big Easy (worsted, 100% cotton, approx. 1¾ oz/50g,
    75⅝ yards/70m), shade 001 White
Size 5mm (H/8) crochet hook (see page 120)
2 pieces of lining material, each 21 x 13½ inches (54 x 34cm)
Matching sewing thread
Sewing needle
Sewing machine
Wooden bag handles, 12½ inches (32cm) wide

MEASUREMENTS
12 inches (30cm) deep, excluding handles.
19 inches (48cm) wide at base.

GAUGE
14 sts per 4 inches (10cm). One complete pattern repeat (bobble plus shell) = approximately 2 inches (5cm), using size 5mm (H/8) crochet hook, or the size to obtain the correct gauge.

ABBREVIATIONS
See page 120.

SPECIAL ABBREVIATIONS
FPdc—front post double crochet: Yarn over hook and insert hook from back to front and right to left over post, or stem, of next stitch in row below, complete double crochet.

BAG

Ch 61.

Row 1: Skip 1 ch, work 1 dc into each ch to end, ch 1, turn.

Rows 2-3: Repeat row 1.

Row 4: ** 1 dc, skip 2 dc, then work 1 FPdc behind the next dc of previous row, work 1 FPdc behind next dc, then work 1 FPdc behind first and then second of the previous 2 dc skipped at the beginning. 1 dc then 8 tr into next dc leaving last loop of each st on hook, draw through all 8 loops (bobble made), ch 1, 1 dc into next dc, repeat from ** to end.

Rows 5-25: Repeat row 4 twenty-one times.

Row 26: 1 dc in each st, ch 1, turn.

Rows 27-28: Repeat row 26 twice.

Fasten off.

LINING

1. Sew ½-inch (1cm) hems along both short sides of each piece.

2. Baste or pin pleats along top and bottom edges of lining to fit crochet bag measurements (see picture opposite).

3. With right sides facing and taking a ½-inch (1cm) seam allowance, sew bottom edges of lining together using the sewing machine. Finish the raw edges with zigzag stitch or make a French seam to enclose raw edges (see page 91).

4. Sew up sides from bottom of bag, stopping 8 inches (20cm) from the top to allow for opening.

5. Place lining in crochet bag, with wrong sides together, and pin sides to opening edges.

6. Turn top edges of lining to wrong side to hide raw edges, adjust to fit, and pin in place; neatly slipstitch top edges of lining and bag together.

7. Pull top of crochet bag through the slots of the handles, and stitch neatly and securely to inside of bag.

8. Close side seams with slipstitch.

9. Work 1 row of bobbles (same as bobble used in main fabric of bag) to both side seams.

Techniques

LIST OF ABBREVIATIONS

beg	begin(ning)
ch	chain
cl	cluster
dc	double crochet
dec	decrease
dtr	double triple
hdc	half-double crochet
inc	increase
rep	repeat
RS	right side
sc	single crochet
sl st(s)	slip stitch(es)
sp(s)	space(s)
st(s)	stitch(es)
tog	together
tr	triple
WS	wrong side
yo	yarn over (hook)

CROCHET HOOKS

The projects in this book were made
using metrically sized crochet hooks,
and we recommend that you use these
also. Comparable American sizes have
been given; however, many of these are
not exact equivalents. Whatever kind of
hook you select, it is usually vital to make
a gauge swatch and, if necessary, change
to a different hook. The gauge—not the
size of the hook—is the crucial factor.

WORKING THE BASIC STITCHES

The patterns in this book assume a basic knowledge of crochet. Absolute beginners should consult a book with a detailed, illustrated introduction to the craft. Here, we give a brief rundown of the basic techniques, followed by the special techniques used for the patterns.

HOLDING THE HOOK AND YARN

There are basically two ways of holding a crochet hook. You can hold it like a knife, with the shaft lying under your palm, or like a pencil, with the shaft lying between your thumb and index finger. In either case, the flat part of the shaft is grasped by the thumb and index finger and the hook itself (when at rest) is facing you.

There are several different ways of holding the yarn. One good way is to take it under, then completely around, the little finger, then over the remaining fingers. The thumb and index finger hold the work and the raised middle finger tensions the yarn.

Beginners tend to work too tightly; if you do this, try to relax.

NOTE For left-handed readers: The words "left" and "right" have been avoided where possible in this section. Where they are used and where a right-handed method of working is shown in the illustrations, you will need to reverse the instructions and images.

WORKING A CHAIN (ABBREVIATION "CH")

Virtually all crochet begins with a slip knot followed by a number of chain stitches, formed by inserting the hook through the slip knot, drawing a loop through and continuing to draw loops through until the required number of chain stitches have been worked.

If you look at the chain you will see that it has two distinct sides: one side—considered the front—is flat; the other has a "bump," formed by the strand leading up to the next link. Normally the hook is inserted under either one or both sides of the front of the chain. Very occasionally you will be told to insert the hook through the "bump" at the back of the work.

NOTE If you need to work a long chain, it is a good idea to leave a fairly long tail 12-16 inches (30-40cm) on the slip knot. If you find, when working the first row, that you've miscounted and are short of chain, you can work some more using this tail. If you have too many, you can unpick them.

OTHER BASIC STITCHES

When working into fabric stitches, as opposed to chain stitches, the hook is normally inserted under both strands of the top of the stitch. At the end of a row, you will need to work one or more chain (called turning chain) to serve as the first stitch of the next row, the number depending on the height of the stitches to be worked in that row.

Slip stitch (abbreviation "sl st")

Insert the hook into the next stitch, draw a loop through both the stitch and the loop on the hook.

This stitch has virtually no height and is used mainly for joining parts of a fabric.

Single crochet (abbreviation "sc")

Insert the hook in the next stitch (or as instructed). Yarn over hook and draw through loop (2 loops on hook). Yarn over hook and draw through both loops.

Number of turning chain: 1.

Half-double crochet (abbreviation "hdc")

Yarn over hook, then insert the hook in the next stitch (or as instructed). Yarn over hook and draw through a loop (3 loops on hook). Yarn over hook and draw through all 3 loops.

Number of turning chain: 2.

Double crochet (abbreviation "dc")

Yarn over hook and insert hook in the next stitch (or as instructed). Yarn over hook and draw through loop (3 loops on hook). Yarn over hook and draw through 2 loops (2 loops on hook). Yarn over hook and draw through 2 loops.

Number of turning chain: 3

Longer stitches are produced by wrapping the yarn over the hook more times before inserting it in the work-for example, 2 times for triple and 3 times for double triple.

KEEPING EDGES STRAIGHT

A common problem for beginners in crochet is managing to keep the edges straight. When starting a new row, make sure you work into the penultimate stitch of the previous row–not into the last one, from which the turning chain emerges. Also remember to work the last stitch of the new row into the turning chain of the previous row.

GAUGE

Whether you crochet loosely or tightly or somewhere in between, it's usually essential to obtain the same gauge–that is, the same number of stitches and rows over a given measurement–as that given with the pattern. A little variation won't matter in the case of a throw or a scarf, but if you're making a fitted garment, working to the wrong gauge could result in a big disappointment: a baggy, shapeless garment or one that's too tight for comfort.

So, before you begin the project, make a swatch to check your gauge. It will be time well spent.

Making a gauge swatch

1   Find out from the pattern the number of stitches and (sometimes) rows to 4 inches (10cm), or other specified measurement, over the stitch pattern.

2   Using a crochet hook of the size recommended for obtaining the correct gauge, make a length of chain adequate to make a swatch 6-8 inches (15-20cm) wide in the stitch pattern.

3   Work enough rows to make the swatch 6-8 inches (15-20cm) deep. Fasten off.

4   Block the swatch (see page 137).

5   Pin the swatch to a towel or flat pad, without stretching.

6   Place a pin between two stitches, a short distance from one edge. Then place a ruler or tape measure along that row, and insert another pin 4 inches (10cm) away from the first pin.

7   Count the number of stitches between the pins.

8   Place a pin between two rows, a short way in from the bottom or top edge. Then place a ruler vertically over the rows, and insert another pin 4 inches (10cm) away from the first pin.

9   Count the number of rows between these pins.

10   Compare your number of stitches and rows with the numbers given in the pattern's gauge measurement. If you have more than the number stated, your crochet is too tight. Make another swatch using a larger hook.

11   If you have fewer rows/stitches than required, your crochet is too loose. Make another swatch using a smaller hook.

SPECIAL STITCHES

LOOPED PUFF STITCH

This stitch produces a softly textured effect, suitable for embellishing an openwork fabric.

1. * Take the yarn over the hook and insert the hook into the chain space below (fig. A).

2. Take the yarn over the hook again and pull the loop through, lifting it up to the required height (3 loops on hook) (fig. B).

3. Repeat from * 3 times (9 loops on hook) (fig. C).

4. Yarn over hook and draw the loop through all 9 loops (fig. D).

5. Yarn over hook and draw it through the loop on the hook to complete the puff stitch. The sample (fig. E) shows 4 completed puff stitches.

A

B

C

D

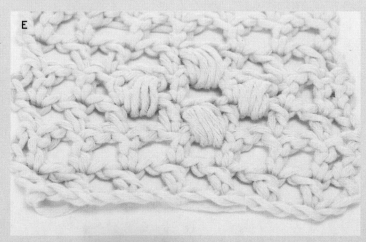

E

A

B

C

CROSSED DOUBLE CROCHET

There are various crochet stitch patterns that involve crossing one stitch over another. The one shown here, which uses double crochet, is one of the simplest. It produces a slightly open fabric with an attractive texture.

1   * Skip the next stitch on the previous row; yarn over hook and work 1 double crochet into the following stitch (fig. A).

2   Work 1 double crochet into the skipped stitch (fig. B). Repeat from * to end.

The sample (fig. C) shows a fabric made of crossed double crochet.

RINGS

A
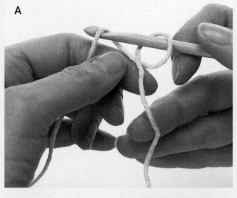

B
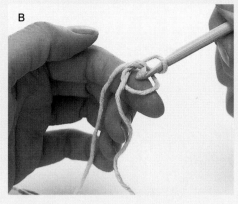

C
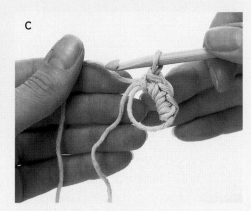

D

E

Closed circle

This method of making a ring is used where you do not want a hole at the center of the work. Practice it using a soft wool yarn, such as knitting worsted, which is easy to manage.

1   Loop the yarn over the hook as shown, with the tail hanging free in front of the loop, and take the other yarn over the hook (fig. A).

2   Draw the yarn through the ring (fig. B). When doing this, you will need to hold the ring quite firmly with your left thumb and index finger to keep it open and prevent it from collapsing.

3   Still holding it firmly (the third finger of your right hand can help with this), work a single crochet over the ring. Note that you will be working over the ring and the tail end of yarn at this point.

4   Continue working single crochet into the ring (fig. C). When you have nearly the required number of stitches, pull gently on the tail yarn to close the ring (fig. D).

5   Work the last two or three stitches, then join the last single crochet to the first one with a slip stitch (fig. E). Continue with the second round as instructed in the pattern.

Open circle

This is an easy ring to make. It is worked over a circle of chain stitches; the fewer the stitches, the smaller the hole.
.

1   Work 5 chain—or the number specified in the pattern.

2   Close the ring with a slipstitch (figs. A and B).

3   Work the specified number of stitches (here single crochet) into the ring (fig. C).

4   Close the first round by working a slip stitch into the first stitch. Then continue with the second round (fig. D) as instructed in the pattern.

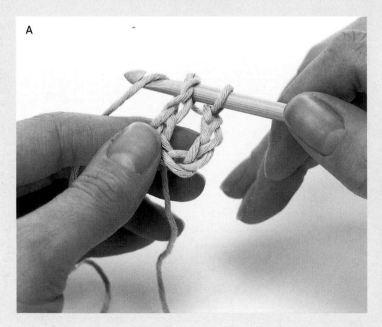

A

B

C

D

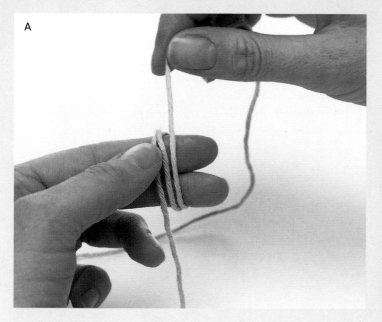

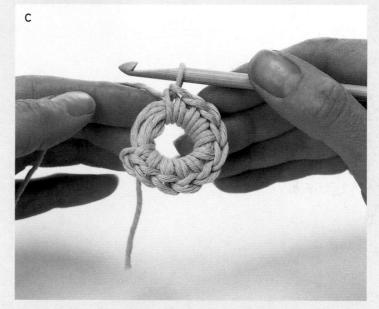

Finger method

This method produces an effect similar to the Open Circle but is preferred where a relatively thick ring is desired at the center.

1   Wind the yarn several times around your first two fingers as shown, leaving the tail of the yarn hanging down in front (fig. A).

2   Remove the yarn ring from your fingers and hold it in your right hand while tensioning the ball end of yarn as usual over your left.

3   Holding the ring with your left thumb and index finger, insert the hook through it; yarn over hook and pull it through the ring. You now have one loop on the hook.

4   Yarn over hook (fig. B) and pull it through this loop.

5   * Insert the hook through the ring. Yarn over hook and pull a loop through the ring (2 loops on hook). Yarn over hook and pull through both loops. One single crochet completed.

6   Repeat from * (fig. C) until ring is covered with single crochet. Trim excess tail just before last stitch; or leave it if required to sew the motif to the main fabric. Close with a slip stitch.

NOTE To make a smaller ring, simply wrap the yarn over only one finger.

MAKING BOBBLES

Many stitch patterns incorporate bobbles, which produce a richly textured fabric. Here is one popular way of making a bobble.

1 * Yarn over the hook and insert the hook into the next stitch. Yarn over hook again and draw a loop through (3 loops on the hook), yarn over hook and draw through first 2 loops (2 loops on hook). * Yarn over hook (fig. A).

2 Inserting the hook into the same place, repeat from * to * 4 more times (number of loops will vary) until you have 6 loops on the hook.

3 Yarn over the hook (fig. B) and draw yarn through all of the loops. Finish the bobble by drawing it through the last loop (fig. C). The sample (fig. D) shows an all-over bobble fabric.

A

B

C

D

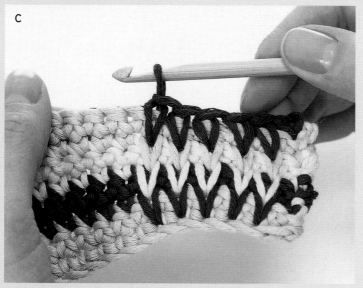

SPIKE STITCH

A huge variety of multicolor effects can be produced with spike stitches. This is not a difficult technique, but achieving the right gauge is crucial; with each stitch the yarn must be brought up to the new working row, without puckering the work. The more rows down the fabric that you work, the more care you must take to keep the fabric flat.

The sample shown includes rows of encroaching spikes, but the basic technique being worked is very simple: each stitch is worked over two previous rows of single crochet.

1   * Insert the hook into the stitch 2 rows down and directly below the stitch to be worked (fig. A).

2   Yarn over the hook and pull a loop through the fabric, drawing it up to the level of the working row (fig. B).

3   Yarn over hook and draw the yarn through the 2 loops on the hook (spike stitch made) (fig. C). Repeat from * to the end.

The sample (fig. D) shows a variety of spike stitches in contrasting colors.

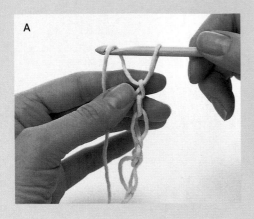

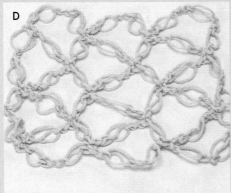

SOLOMON'S KNOT

Although it's rather tricky to master, Solomon's Knot (which is known by various other names, including Knot Stitch and Lover's Knot) is well worth the effort. It produces a wonderfully lacy mesh, suitable for all sorts of things, from scarves to string bags to curtains.

First row
Begin, as usual, with a slip knot on the hook. (Several knots have previously been completed in this sample.)

1   Make 1 chain and draw it up to the required length (typically about ¾ inch [2cm]).
2   * Yarn over hook (fig. A) and draw it through long loop. This produces an extra, long strand behind the long loop.
3   Holding this strand away from the loop with your left thumb and index finger, twist the hook in front of the loop and under this strand (fig. B), then catch the tensioned working thread and draw it through the strand (2 loops on hook).
4   Yarn over hook and draw it through first loop (fig. C) and then second loop. Pull loop up to same height (¾ inch [2cm]) as in step 1 (1 Solomon's Knot made). Repeat from * until you have the required (even) number of knots.

Second row
1   Skip the next 3 knots from the hook and work a single crochet into the center of the next knot.
2   * Extend the loop on the hook and make 2 Solomon's Knots, each about half again as long as those in the first row.
3   Skip the next knot in the base row, and work a single crochet into the center of the next knot. Repeat to the end of the row.

Third row
1   Make 3 knots. Work a single crochet into the center of the next free knot of the previous row.
2   * Make 2 knots. Work a single crochet into the center of the next free knot of the previous row. Repeat from * to the end of the row.

Repeating the third row forms the pattern (fig. D).

JACQUARD CROCHET

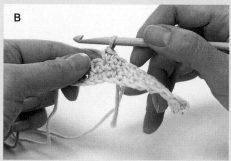

Also called intarsia, jacquard crochet is a method of producing a multicolored fabric in which colors are changed within a row or round (as opposed to a horizontally striped flat fabric, in which they are changed at the beginning of a row). There are several ways of achieving this.

If only two colors are being used, and are changed at frequent intervals (as in narrow vertical stripes), the color not in use at any given time may be carried along the back of the work and simply crocheted over using the working yarn. This will, however, produce a denser fabric.

To prevent the old color from encroaching on the new one, it's important to change to the new one when completing the stitch just before the actual color change. For example:

Changing color in single crochet

1 Insert the hook into the last stitch before the color change, take the yarn over the hook and pull through (2 loops on hook).
2 Holding the old color out of the way with your working hand, pick up the new one and take it over the hook (fig. A); pull it through both loops, completing both stitch and color change.
3 Continue working with the new color, at the same time carrying the old color along the row (fig. B). On both right-side and wrong-side rows, take the hook under the unused color before working the stitch in the color being used.

The sample (fig. C) shows a finished piece of jacquard crochet.

NOTE When you have changed to the new color, you will need to pull the old yarn slightly to tighten the stitch a little. But avoid pulling it taut when carrying it across the back; otherwise the work will pucker.

Changing color in double crochet

1 Take the yarn over the hook and insert the hook into the last stitch before the color change. Yarn over hook and pull a loop through (3 loops on hook).

2 Yarn over hook and pull a loop through first 2 loops on hook.
3 Holding the old color out of the way with your working hand, pick up the new color and pull it through the last 2 loops to complete the double crochet. The color change is completed. Carry the old yarn along the work as described for single crochet.

Working with separate lengths of yarn

Where several colors are being used; where the change of color is widely spaced; where there is a possibility of unused colors showing through on the right side; or where a denser fabric is undesirable, it is necessary to use separate balls of yarn. To prevent a tangle of yarns, it's advisable to wind lengths of the different colors onto plastic bobbins (available from needlecraft shops). Most important: when changing from one color to another, you must cross the yarns over each other on the wrong side; otherwise a slit will result along the color change. When first introducing a new yarn (called B), simply knot them together. Change colors as described above, but leave the first one (called A) hanging loose. On the next (wrong-side) row, when you reach the last stitch before changing back to yarn A,

1 Work this stitch in yarn B but do not complete it.
2 Allow yarn B to fall down along the wrong side of the work, and bring yarn A under yarn B and over it.
3 Complete the stitch using yarn A. The two yarns have been crossed.

On the following (right-side) row complete the last stitch before the color change in yarn B, first letting yarn A drop down on the wrong side and bringing yarn B under, then over it. After several rows, you will see that the yarns are twisted around each other, as a result of being crossed on each row.

Whichever method you are using, you will have some loose ends on the wrong side. When the crochet is finished, use a tapestry needle to darn these in neatly on the wrong side.

EDGINGS AND EMBELLISHMENTS

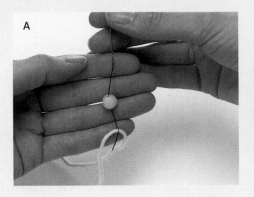

WORKING WITH BEADS (ABOVE)

The addition of beads to a crocheted fabric will add texture and—in some cases—glamour. The best fabric for bead work is single crochet, which is solid enough to prevent the beads from slipping through to the wrong side and strong enough to bear their weight.

1 Thread a sewing needle with a short length of thread, double it, and knot the ends. Slip one end of the yarn through the thread, and thread the required number of beads onto the yarn as shown (fig. A).

2 Add the beads while working a wrong-side row. At the point for adding each bead, insert the hook into the next stitch, yarn over hook and draw loop through (2 loops on hook).

3 Push a bead up close to the hook. Yarn over hook (fig. B) and draw through both loops, completing a single crochet. Tighten the stitch if necessary to ensure that bead sits on the other (right) side of the fabric. The sample (fig. C) shows the completed bead work.

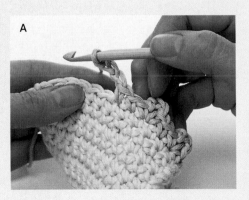

PICOT EDGING (ABOVE)

Picots are neat little points, made of short lengths of chain forming a loop. They have a variety of uses. Sometimes they form part of a lacy stitch pattern, but more often they're used in edgings. The method described below produces a simple edging in which picots alternate with single crochet.

1 Fasten the yarn at one corner of the fabric. Work 1 single crochet into first stitch.

2 * Work 3 chain stitches (fig. A).

3 Slip stitch into same stitch (picot made) (fig. B).

4 Work 1 single crochet into next two stitches. Repeat from * to end. If desired, the picots can be spaced out along the edge, with more single crochet worked in between them. The sample (fig. C) shows the completed picot edging.

A

B

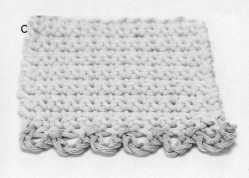

C

OPEN PICOT EDGING (ABOVE)

Open picots produce a lacier edging than normal picots. In the example shown here, they are joined to every alternate stitch of the main fabric.

1   Fasten the yarn at one corner. * Work 4 chain stitches (fig. A).

2   Skip 1 stitch, 1 single crochet into next stitch (fig. B). Repeat from * to end.

The sample (fig. C) shows the completed open picot edging.

A

B

C

SHELL EDGING (ABOVE)

This scalloped edging is particularly attractive when worked in a color contrasting with the main fabric, though it can equally well be worked in the same color. The fabric edge should consist of a multiple of 4 stitches, plus 1 extra stitch at the end.

1   Begin by fastening the yarn to the first stitch at the edge of the fabric. * Skip the next stitch and work 5 double crochet (fig. A–3 completed here) into the following stitch.

2   Skip the next stitch and work 1 single crochet into the following stitch (fig. B). Repeat from * along the edge of the fabric, ending with a single crochet into the last stitch. The sample (fig. C) shows the completed open picot edging.

If continuing the edging along the adjacent vertical edge, keep the spacing the same. A row of single crochet, worked in the main fabric yarn, will provide a better foundation for the edging.

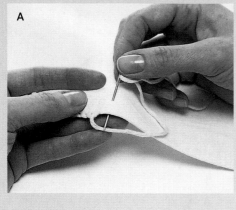

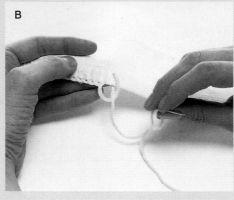

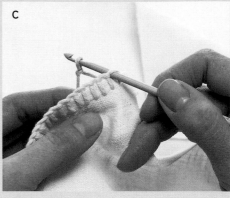

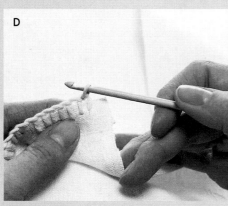

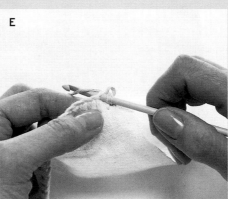

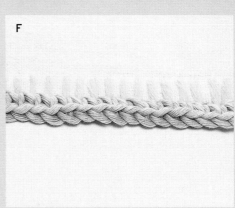

BLANKET STITCH WITH SINGLE CROCHET EDGING

This method—which can be varied by means of different crochet stitches—is used where you wish to apply a crochet edging to a piece of woven fabric. You will need a sharp-pointed embroidery needle, such as a chenille needle, with an eye large enough for your chosen yarn or thread. It's a good idea to practice this technique on a spare piece of fabric, in order to get the spacing correct.

1   Fasten the yarn on the wrong side of the fabric, close to the edge. With the right side of the fabric facing you, insert the needle a short distance to the right, at the desired height of the stitch, and bring it up over the thread at the lower edge (fig. A). Pull the thread through gently, so that the loop sits on the edge of the fabric.

2   Continue in this way, spacing the stitches evenly along the fabric edge (fig. B). Do not pull the thread too tightly. When the stitching is complete, fasten off the thread on the wrong side.

3   Insert the crochet hook through the first blanket stitch as shown, and place a slip knot on it. (fig. C).

4   Draw the loop through the edge of the blanket stitch (fig. D).

5   * Insert the hook into the next blanket stitch; yarn over hook and draw a loop through. (fig. E).

6   Yarn over hook and through both loops on hook-one single crochet completed. Repeat from * to the end of the row. Fasten off.

The sample (fig. F) shows the completed edging.

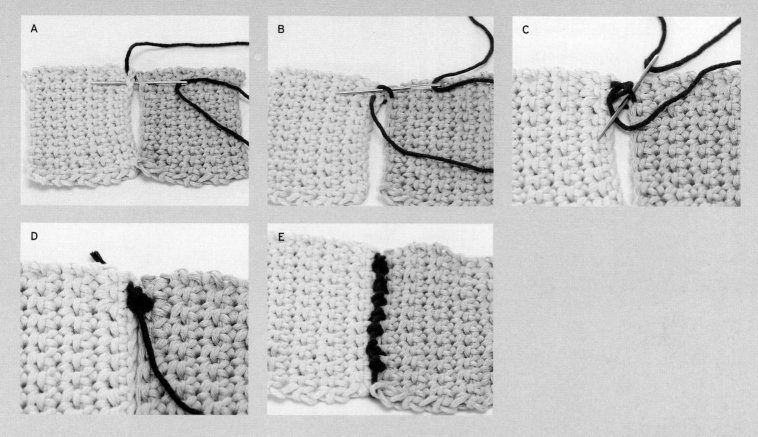

DOUBLE KNOT STITCH

This is a decorative way of joining two pieces of crochet, especially suitable for a blanket or other household accessory. Work the stitching with a tapestry needle, so as not to split the embroidered or crocheted stitches.

1   Place the motifs side by side, with right sides facing upward.

2   Fasten the embroidery thread with a couple of backstitches on the wrong side of the left-hand piece, and bring it through to the right side of the fabric, close to the corner.

3   * Insert the needle in the right-hand piece, a short distance down, and bring it up in the left-hand piece, exactly opposite (fig. A). Pull the thread through. This forms a small diagonal stitch linking the two pieces.

4   Slip the needle under this stitch from right to left, without entering the crochet fabric (fig. B). Pull the thread through, but not too tightly, to form the first part of the knot.

5   Loop the thread counterclockwise below the stitch, and take the needle under the stitch again, then over the loop (fig. C). Pull gently to complete the knot (fig. D). Repeat steps from * to the end.

The sample (fig. E) shows a completed row of double knot stitch.

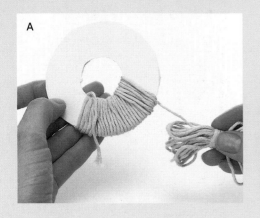
A

B

C

POMPOMS

You can buy forms for making pompoms at needlework shops. Alternatively, you can use circles cut from cardboard. Use an object of the required diameter (such as a cosmetics jar) as a template. Draw around it twice on a piece of cardboard, and cut out the two circles. In the center of one circle, draw a smaller circle, about one-third to one-half the diameter of the outer circle. The thicker the yarn, the larger the inner circle should be. Measure inward at several points to make sure the circle is centered. Cut out the inner circle. Place the completed circle over the other circle and trace the inner circle. Cut this out.

1   Place the two rings together and wind yarn over them (fig. A) until the center hole is nearly full.

2   Cut around the edge of the two rings.

3   Wind a length of yarn between the cardboard circles, then remove them. Tie the yarn tightly around the cut threads (fig. B). Leave the long ends for sewing the pompom to the crocheted item.

4   Fluff out the threads to finish the pompom (fig. C). If any threads stick out, trim the ends.

CURLICUE TASSEL

Begin by making the required length of chain. This will usually be stated in the pattern. If not, or if you are designing your own curlicue tassel, experiment to find a suitable length.

1   Into the 2nd chain from the hook work 1 single crochet, 1 half-double crochet, and 1 double crochet.

2   * Into the next chain work at least 4 double crochet. Repeat from * along the length of the chain. Use the working yarn to fasten the curlicue to the edge of the fabric, as shown (see fig. A), with a slip stitch or single crochet, then use a tapestry needle to darn the ends into the tassel or the edge of the fabric.

Note that the more double crochet you work into the chain, the more the tassel will curl.

A

FINISHING

BLOCKING

To block a piece of crocheted fabric, you pin it out to the correct size and shape, then press or damp-finish it. The blocked pieces are then sewn together. Blocking gives a smooth finish and proper shape to the crocheted fabric, stretching edges that are pulling, sharpening points and corners, and drawing buttonhole slits together.

Blocking is done on a blocking pad laid on a firm, flat surface, such as an ironing board, kitchen table, or floor. The blocking pad should be fairly thick; a large folded clean towel or an old blanket covered with a white cloth will suffice. Pins should be rustless and have glass or other highly visible heads. Err on the side of generosity when using the pins.

Read the yarn label to check the pressing instructions for the yarn. If using more than one yarn, follow the gentlest method of pressing or use the damp-finishing method, described below. Do not press highly textured stitch patterns. Damp finishing is recommended for the novice or the nervous.

Pinning out

With the wrong side of the crochet uppermost, pin out each piece along the edges to size and shape, making sure that the rows and the columns of stitches are straight. The pins should be at right angles to the fabric.

Pressing

1   Cover the crocheted piece with a white cloth. As a general rule, use a dry cloth for synthetics and a damp cloth for natural fibers, both with a dry iron. Be guided by the pressing instructions on the yarn label.

2   Heat the iron to the correct temperature, as stated on the yarn label.

3   Put the iron on the cloth and immediately lift it up again. Repeat all over the crocheted piece. Never use an ironing motion.

4   Leave the cloth in place until cool and/or dry.

Damp finishing

1   Fill a spray bottle with cold water, and lightly spray the crocheted piece until damp.

2   Cover with a clean white cloth, and pat gently to absorb excess water.

3   Remove the cloth and allow the crocheted piece to dry naturally.

SEAMS

Before joining pieces of crochet, darn in any loose ends on the wrong side of the work.

There are various ways of joining the pieces. They may be placed wrong side up on a flat surface and sewn together edge to edge, using whip stitch and working the stitches through one loop only of each edge. Or they can be placed together with right sides facing and joined with crochet, using slip stitches. If the edges are uneven and a strong join is required, you can sew them, right sides together, with backstitch, using a tapestry needle. For a decorative effect, you can place them together with wrong sides facing and work single crochet over the two edges, using a contrasting color. Or join the seams with Double Knot Stitch.

Suppliers

YARN

Listed below are the manufacturers and suppliers of the yarns used in this book. These companies generally sell their products exclusively to yarn and crafts retailers. Please contact them to locate the retailers nearest you that carry their products..

Be Sweet
1315 Bridgeway, Sausalito, CA 94965
Tel: 415 331 9676
www.besweetproducts.com

Blue Sky Alpacas
P.O. Box 88
Cedar, MN 55011
Tel: 888 460 8862
www.blueskyalpacas.com

Jade Sapphire
148 Germonds Road, West Nyack, NY 10994
Tel: 866 857 3897
www.jadesapphire.com

Knitting Fever, Inc.
315 Bayview Avenue, Amityville, NY 11701
Tel: 800 645 3457
www.knittingfever.com
Debbie Bliss and Louisa Harding yarns.

Lana Grossa
Heritage Stitchcraft,
Redrook Lane,
Rugeley,
Staffordshire
WS15 1QU, UK
Tel: +44 (0)1889 585 666
www.lanagrossa.com

Muench Yarns, Inc.
1323 Scott Street,
Petaluma, CA 94954
Tel: 800 733 9276
www.muenchyarns.com
ggh yarns.

pear tree
P.O. Box 463, Torquay, Victoria, Australia 3228
Tel: +61 03 5261 6375
www.peartreeproducts.com

Texere Yarns
College Mill, Barkerend Road, Bradford, West Yorkshire BD1 4AU, UK
Tel: +44 (0)1274 722 191
www.texere.co.uk
Yarns and supplies for knitting, sewing, felt-making, and weaving.

Westminster Fibers, Inc.
18 Celina Avenue #17,
Nashua, NH 03063
Tel: 800 445 9276
www.westminsterfibers.com
Rowan and Jaeger yarns.

FABRICS

In addition to using fabric to line bags or purses, or as an edging for a blanket or throw, you can also crochet with it. Cut or rip the fabric into narrow strips and tie these into a ball of "yarn" to work with. It takes a surprisingly large number of strips to make up enough to work with, so buy more fabric than you think you will need. If your project requires only a small amount of fabric, consider using vintage clothes or curtains. Fabric strips and ribbons also look lovely threaded through crocheted pieces, especially the more open crochet stitches.

A huge variety of fabric is available from crafts stores, while lovely vintage fabrics may be found at flea markets, second-hand shops, textile fairs, and on the Internet.

reprodepot.com
www.reprodepot.com
Reproductions of vintage fabric.

EMBELLISHMENTS AND EXTRAS

Turkish "Oya" lace flowers
Available from a variety of online sources and Loop (see below). The history of the decorative edging known in Europe as "Turkish lace" dates back to the 8th century BC. These needle-lace flowers are made in villages across Turkey, traditionally by farming women, who used them to decorate their scarves. They are charming threaded together in clusters as an embellishment or trim.

Buttons
Besides being functional, buttons can be used as embellishments. You can use one stunning huge one with other smaller elements (such as small buttons, tiny pompoms, or beads), or use beautiful vintage buttons in clusters or scattered along an edge. For unusual or vintage examples, try vintage-textile shows, which are usually advertised in local antiques papers or craft and textile magazines. You can also mooch around flea markets, rummage sales, and secondhand shops. It's often worth looking at secondhand clothing to see if the buttons are interesting—you can cut them off and use them for your new piece. Ebay is also a good source.

Beads

There are many sources for beads: local yarn and craft stores, online retailers, and mail-order catalogs. The choices are infinite.

Purse clasps and bag handles and frames

Lacis

3163 Adeline Street, Berkeley, CA 94703

Tel: 510 843 7178

www.lacis.com

Fabulous selection of the most exquisite bag and purse frames and handles. They have vintage Lucite and other beauties.

Pillow forms

Standard-size pillow forms can be found at crafts and fabric stores. There are also online retailers who offer custom sizes and specialty shapes.

AUTHOR CONTACT

Loop

41 Cross Street, Islington, London N1 2BB, UK

Tel: +44 (0)20 7288 1160

www.loop.gb.com

All of the yarns and crochet supplies shown in this book are available at Loop and from Loop's online shop. We ship worldwide.

PROP CREDITS

The publisher and author would also like to thank the following individuals and companies for kindly lending props for the photoshoot:

Julie Arkell "Trolley Creature"

(as seen on page 99).

Wide selection available at Loop and at Flow Gallery, 1–5 Needham Road, London W11 2RP, UK

Tel: +44 (0)20 7243 0782

www.flowgallery.co.uk

Caravan

11 Lamb Street, Old Spitalfields Market, London E1 6EA, UK

Tel:+ 44 (0)20 7247 6467

www.caravanstyle.com

An eclectic and unusual mix for the home and to wear. Caravan offers a wide range of new and old pieces. Stock includes hand-knitted toys for cats, vintage teapots, brightly colored industrial-style lighting, and skirts crafted from vintage floral fabrics.

Gladys Carvell cardigan by Keep & Share

(as seen on page 115).

Available at Loop and at Keep & Share, Lugwardine Court, Lugwardine, Hereford HR1 4AE, UK

Tel: +44 (0)1432 851 162

www.keepandshare.co.uk

Hannah Lamb

16a Ashfield Terrace, Bingley, West Yorkshire BD16 1EQ, UK

Tel: +44 (0)1274 781346

www.hannahlamb.co.uk

Carefully detailed, beautifully handmade accessories. Hannah creates practical pieces for the home and to wear, from a carefully planned combination of nostalgic ephemera.

Life's a Picnic

Contact Elly and Evie Pace

Tel: +44 (0)20 7790 0335/ +44 (0)7966 149533

www.lifesapicnic.co.uk

Luncheon hampers that are classy, fun and totally individual. Willow picnic hampers lined with vintage fabrics and fully fitted with vintage tableware and linen.

Amy Ruppel paintings

(as seen on pages 7 and 52).

Available at Loop and at www.amyruppel.com

These are made by the lovely Amy Ruppel in Portland, Oregon, by mixing pigment with encaustic resin and beeswax applied to wood. They are the only thing I sell at Loop that has absolutely nothing to do with knitting or crochet, but they make me happy. Some people say that the nests remind them of balls of yarn, so there you go.

Contributing Designers

BEE CLINCH has always been fascinated by the wonder of handmade objects—from a rag rug to a swatch of sixties floral fabric to a seventies mohair sweater. As she grew up, first in California and then in England, Bee became obsessed with the variety of textures and colors of yarn and how it can be transformed with crochet into something wonderful.

Bee is determined to show that everyone can enjoy the versatility of crochet, and through her design work and teaching, she is able to pursue her love for the craft and explore this potentially endless expression of creativity.
www.bee-at-home.co.uk

KRISTEEN GRIFFIN-GRIMES is a designer based in Washington State and creator of French Girl's hallmark style of knit and crochet patterns: ethereal, draped garments superbly fitting to the feminine form. French Girl patterns are constructed in a unique manner: the garments fashioned in one piece from start to finish. Using her seamstress and costuming background, Kristeen begins her design process almost architecturally, to deconstruct her envisioned garment and reconstruct it again in a more organic way, either from the top down, from the hem up, or from the back out.

The designer's aesthetic is rooted in her early years as a "nature girl" on her family's oyster farm on the rural Pacific Northwest coast.
www.frenchgirlknits.com

BOBBI INTVELD Bobbi IntVeld was born and raised in Minnesota. She began working in her grandmother's yarn shop in White Bear Lake at the age of 12, and very soon learned to knit, crochet, and design her own patterns.

Bobbi is now an enthusiastic designer, who has had both knit and crochet patterns published. She also teaches, aiming to pass on her love for these crafts to others.

KATE JENKINS worked as a knitwear consultant for various fashion houses, including Marc Jacobs and Donna Karan, before founding her own company, Cardigan, in 2003. With a strong emphasis on color and innovative quirky details, Cardigan has become synonymous with the creation of beautiful knitted and crocheted accessories. Cardigan's philosophy is that anything can be knitted as long as the products are made with love.

2006 saw the opening of Cardigan's first studio shop in Brighton, England, where customers can view the entire Cardigan collection and see the beautiful studio where the designs are created.
www.cardigan.ltd.uk

CLAIRE MONTGOMERIE has an M. A. in Constructed Textiles from the Royal College of Art, London. She has a wealth of experience in the craft and textile industries and runs a successful online business selling her quirky knitted wares. Claire teaches knitting classes at Loop, children's textile courses at the artsdepot, London, and textile jewely courses at West Dean College, Sussex.

Claire is the author of *Easy Baby Knits* and the co-author of *London Crochet*. She has also contributed designs to *Hookorama, Instant Expert Crochet,* and *Loop: Pretty Knits.*
www.clairemontgomerie.com

ALICIA PAULSON Alicia Paulson is a designer of handmade products and crochet-wear who lives in Portland, Oregon, in a house filled with pets, flowers, and far too much yarn. She writes daily on her blog (aliciapaulson.com) about life, love, and all things crafty and is working on a book of memory-inspired sewing projects. Her small collection of one-of-a-kind handmade accessories and crochet patterns is available from her website.
www.rosylittlethings.com.

LEIGH RADFORD is an award-winning author, designer, and teacher living in the Pacific Northwest. Her books include the highly popular *AlterKnits: Imaginative Projects and Creativity Exercises* and *One Skein: 30 Quick Projects to Knit & Crochet.*

In 2006 Leigh created Silk Gelato, a ribbon yarn offering knitters a fiber with enhanced texture and rich color for her unique pattern designs. Her enterprising efforts have resulted in a highly successful business collaboration with Lantern Moon, producers of Silk Gelato.

Leigh is in demand for her innovative classes and workshops. She enjoys teaching others the value of being creative and is inspired by the expression of original ideas that lend a fresh perspective to knitting and crochet.
www.leighradford.com

KATE SAMPHIER was inspired by traditional knitting in Scotland, and her collections embrace Scottish knitwear manufacture, challenging tradition with an eclectic use of color, texture, and pattern.

After studying textiles in the Scottish Borders, Kate worked for a local woollen spinner for five years as a yarn and knit-fabric designer. Drawn to the raw material and colors that she worked with, Kate began to create her own knitted accessories to illustrate the versatility of the company's yarn ranges.

In Spring 2000 Kate set up her design studio and workshop. The following year her first collection of knitted accessories was launched. Featured in magazines such as *Easy Living*, *Homes and Gardens*, *Junior*, and *Selvedge*, Kate's designs are for women with an eye for beauty and a quirky sense of style.
www.katesamphier.co.uk

EMMA SEDDON was taught to knit by her grandmother, and has never looked back. She trained at Central St Martins School of Art, in London, where she did a Knitted Textiles degree. Working for the next 12 years on a variety of different textiles products, she spent most of her free time knitting, crocheting, and sewing, taking the occasional spare moment to peruse thrift shops for patterns and balls of yarn.

In 2004 she became freelance, to pursue her first loves of knitting and crochet and to inspire others to do the same, through teaching. She works with Rowan as a freelance design consultant, teaches at local schools of higher education, and works on a wide range of design projects.

NICKI TRENCH founded Laughing Hens, a British mail-order knitting Web site, which has captured a new wave of interest in knitting as a modern creative hobby for women. Nicki has written two books, *The Cool Girl's Guide to Knitting* and *The Cool Girl's Guide to Crochet*, and is currently writing a third, *The Cool Girl's Guide to Sewing*.

Nicki's inspiration has always been color and texture, and she loves vintage designs in fabric and textile. The flowers, dots, and stripes represented in her designs draw on 1950s retro and 1960s color. Her background in wedding-cake design is reflected in her hand knitting and crochet—opulent big roses and pretty, delicate flowers and leaves in yummy colorful yarns that look good enough to eat.
www.laughinghens.com

JUJU VAIL came to the U. K. in 1990 to study for an M. A. in Textile Design at Central St Martins School of Art, in London, after studying fashion and knitwear design in Montreal. Since graduating, she has taught and written books and articles on many creative practices. These include quilting, sewing, beading, knitting, crochet, painting, and rug making.

Juju has a whim of iron and chronicles her creative passions on her blog. Her latest book is *Creative Beadwork*.
www.jujulovespolkadots.typepad.com

Acknowledgments

This book was blessed with a wonderful team of talented people, who were all a joy to work with. It was so important to me that, besides being chock-full of really great patterns, the book should have a cozy, beautiful warmth. All of the people involved helped realize that dream for me, and I thank them all.

First and foremost I wish to express my thanks to all the talented designers, both in Britain and in the United States, who have contributed their creativity and sensibility to this project. That they took time out of their already very hectic lives has truly touched me. Each of them is taking crochet in a wonderful direction and inspiring a new generation of people to take up the craft, by making it inspiring and exciting.

Thanks to Kristin Perers. Her incredible eye and artisan spirit inform all of the images. In addition to taking the beautiful photographs, she tweaked and fiddled until everything was "just so"; and the care she took is obvious in every frame. Thank you, also, to Heather Lewin, Kristin's brilliant assistant.

A huge "thank you" to sweet Emily Chalmers. Her quirky sense of style is enchanting and I feel honored to have had her work on this project. Like a magpie, she swoops on everyday things and finds some unique beauty in them. From cupcakes to dog trolleys, she left no stone unturned.

Thanks to both Emily and Debi Treloar for the use of their charming homes, which were like treasure troves, and to Bee Clinch for her peaceful "country spread."

Thanks to the lovely Lucy Chapman and Rosie Doren, who modeled the garments so professionally; and to Emma Seddon, who swatched everything for the techniques section.

Also, a big "thank you" to Zia Mattocks, my commissioning editor, who, with her cool head, kept things ticking at all times. Thanks also to Barbara Zuñiga, our book designer, whom, once again, I had the great fortune to have on this project. And, of course, to Jacqui Small, who thought of the book in the first place. Thank you for approaching Loop and believing in the book and making it happen.

Thanks to Blue Sky Alpacas, Designer Yarns (for Debbie Bliss and Louisa Harding's yarns), ggh, Rowan, Jaeger, pear tree, Jade Sapphire, Lana Grossa, and Be Sweet for their support and generosity (and for making such beautiful yarns!).

My heartfelt thanks to the incredible staff at Loop. I have been lucky enough, right from the beginning, to have warm, responsible, helpful people, who happen to be great at knitting and crochet as well. Thank you to Linda Marveng, Claire Montgomerie, and Stefan Reekie. Your grace and enthusiasm for the craft have made the shop an everyday joy and the book possible. Also thanks to our talented teachers, whose patience, together with their passion for knitting and crochet, is truly inspiring: Bee Clinch, Emma Seddon, Juju Vail, Aneeta Patel, Laura Long, Julie Arkell, Jane Lithgow, and, of course, Linda and Claire. Thank you to Emerald Mosley, my ever-faithful Web site designer, who makes it so beautiful.

And also, thank you to all Loop's customers—your enthusiasm for the craft keeps it all fresh and exciting, and is the reason we are here.

To Joy, who likes to mooch around the yarn fairs with me and makes samples for the shop, and my dad, Jack Silverberg—thank you both for all of the kind support you have given. And my brother, David, who sends me messages from faraway places and a heads-up when he discovers anyone involved in textiles who he thinks might inspire me.

Thanks to my mom, Joan Podel, who dragged me around the museums and design fairs of New York as a child and through osmosis gave me a passion for design and simple beauty. Those yarns hanging in our bathroom for your weaving in the seventies must have seeped into my system. A heartfelt thanks for your unwavering enthusiasm for everything that I ever do, and for Loop.

I couldn't have done any of this book without the huge support on the home front from my dear husband, Steven, and our three beautiful children, Sonia, Niall, and Jonah. They have been generous beyond belief and endlessly patient with me and the piles of yarns, hooks, needles, ribbons, buttons, stacks of papers, and scribbled notes and Polaroids stuck on walls, which have graced our home over the course of the year. I know you will secretly miss it all.

Index